JED TALKS #1

ESSAYS, TEACHINGS, RANTS
&
FRIVOLOUS FRIVOLITY

2ND EDITION

JED MCKENNA

Jed Talks #1

Essays, Teachings, Rants & Frivolous Frivolity

2nd Edition

Jed McKenna

Print ISBN: 978-0-9714352-8-5

E-Book ISBN: 978-0-9978797-3-5

Contents

No problem can withstand the
assault of sustained thinking.

Voltaire

Toe Jam

How old would you be if you
didn't know how old you are?

Satchel Paige

*Jed and Douglas sit facing each other. Douglas, 30, sits
cross-legged and barefoot. We join them in mid-conversation.*

DOUGLAS
But I'm a good person. I don't hurt anyone, I
give money to charity, I go to church. Doesn't
that count for anything?

JED
That's a good question for you to pursue using
the process of spiritual autolysis, I'd say. A good
starting point.

DOUGLAS

What? Whether being a good person should count for something?

JED

Whether *any*thing counts for anything. Ask yourself what you mean by that. Count for what? Count with whom? What is this entity or organization that you think is keeping track of you? Who are you performing for? Who is your audience?

DOUGLAS

Are you asking me?

JED

I'm suggesting you ask yourself.

DOUGLAS

God? Karma? I don't know.

JED

I know you don't know, but *you* don't know you don't know. This is an example of a shadow demon. You are engulfed in shadows and your mind plays tricks on you. You see vague shapes and your mind interprets them as real things. That's what the spiritual autolysis process is for, to light up these dark areas of your universe where you think you see something lurking, and seeing clearly that there's nothing there, which, by the way, there never is.

DOUGLAS

How does that help?

JED

Lighting up your interior universe is… Are you really gonna make me say it?

DOUGLAS

Say what? Oh, enlightening? Oh yeah, okay, sorry, I get it. So what do I do? I just start writing? Or I write out a question and try to answer it or something?

JED

You do it however you do it, however you can, written or verbal, whatever works for you. Give it some context and subtext. Write as if corresponding with the past you or your future child. Write it out like a sermon or a speech. Write to me or Krishna or your dead mother, whatever, as long as it helps you achieve focus.

DOUGLAS

So, like journaling?

JED

If I were suggesting that you try to get in touch with your feelings, I might suggest journaling, but I don't give a shit about your feelings and neither should you. I'm suggesting you bring your brain fully online and start making it work for you. Your ability to think is your number one asset and you don't even know how to do it. No offense, not your fault. Your only hope in waking up is your ability to think, not your ability to explore your feelings or devote yourself to a guru or exhibit compassion. You have to think clearly and coldly, and no else can do it for you. There's a million ways to make believe you're awake, and you can convince others too because what they hell do they know?, but there's only one way out of the sleeping dream-state and that's with the power of the focused mind.

DOUGLAS

You make it sound like a war.

JED

Not *a* war, *the* war. The internal conflict between dark and light is the only real war there is. Everything else is just puppets and shadowplay. Your eyes are shut tight so you see the world as the soft blur of light and dark visible through closed eyelids. You can't see anything clearly so you can only guess what's out there. It's not wrong or evil, it's just the way life is with closed eyes. But now we're talking about going inside and lighting the place up, destroying darkness with light, destroying ignorance with clear seeing. Look everywhere, see everything, believe nothing. It can be done, but it's a process. Naturally, it will result in your becoming a totally different being in a totally different world.

DOUGLAS

Enlightened.

JED

We can't avoid saying so. Another way to say it is that, by coming to me, you are asking me to cut your head off, but I can't do that for you. Only you can do it.

DOUGLAS

And what if I don't want to cut my head off?

JED

Then don't. But in that case, you're talking to the exact wrong person. I am the teacher of self-decapitation. It's all I got.

DOUGLAS

They say it's good to specialize.

JED

They are wise.

DOUGLAS

Still, I'm not sure this is what I'm looking for.

JED

I'm sure it's not, but this is what you've found. Pay attention to things like that.

DOUGLAS

Are you saying…?

JED

I'm saying you can learn to open your eyes and see for yourself because whatever you ask, that's always my answer. Ask me the time, it's time to open your eyes.

DOUGLAS

And spiritual autolysis will do that?

JED

Thinking will do that, but you have to begin by developing focus and igniting intent. That's what the writing process will help with. And then the focus and intent will help intensify the autolysis and they'll keep feeding each other and the next thing you know, you're actually taking an actual step, and the journey of awakening is never anything more than taking the next step. Further.

DOUGLAS

And that's what you think I should do?

JED

No, I think you should go have a family and be a Christian or a Buddhist or something safe and forget all about this waking up stuff. It's life-denying. What's the point of that?

DOUGLAS

But you're an enlightenment teacher.

JED

Yeah, kind of, but what if I was a jump-on-a-grenade teacher? It doesn't mean I think everyone should want to go around jumping on grenades all the time. Jumping on grenades is a very limited field of endeavor based on a very specific set of circumstances that few people will ever need to even contemplate. At least, I hope not.

It would be a pretty messed up world if every-one needed a jump-on-a-grenade teacher.

DOUGLAS

I've never met a teacher like you. You're a very strange person.

JED

Ha! You think I'm strange? You should see my toes.

DOUGLAS

Why, are your toes strange?

JED

All toes are strange. Don't get me started. Never mind, sorry I mentioned it. Just my own little bugaboo. We all have our pet peeves, I guess. Some people have a thing about ending world hunger or creating world peace, some people have a thing about toes. Really, don't get me started.

DOUGLAS

Okay.

JED

I mean, seriously though, what the hell are they? Shrunken little foot-fingers, right? They don't do shit, they look freaky, they hurt like hell when you stub them, they're hard to main-tain, and although mine are quite attractive, most people's are totally disgusting.

DOUGLAS

Okay, okay, I'm sorry I asked.

JED

Yours are disgusting. Look at those stupid things. Seriously, you never thought about toes? Maybe that's where you should start your autolysis. Get your head right about this whole toe thing. Toes? I mean, claws, okay, I can see that. At least they do something, right? Maybe help you climb or dig or defend yourself or something, but what do toes do? Nothing. They just sit there and look stupid. Oh, sorry, they curl. Wow, how great is that?

DOUGLAS

Yeah, I don't know.

JED

Of course you don't, no one does. If I didn't have this enlightenment thing going, I'd be out campaigning to raise awareness about how stupid toes are. Completely unnecessary. Total design flaw. Somebody got tired toward the end of creating humans and just gave up. That's the guy I want to talk to; lazy-ass bastard, stupid toe inventor. It's not even an invention, it's just like, "Oh wow, what am I gonna do at the end of the foot? Oh, I know, I'll just copy and paste some fingers and then shrink them down to useless little nubs." Yeah, good work. Thanks buddy. Thanks for sticking a bunch of useless little fingers on the end of my foot. Now I gotta be a circus freak because you can't do your job.

DOUGLAS

We all have toes.

JED

Like that makes it okay?

DOUGLAS

Are you teaching me something right now?

JED

Yeah, I'm teaching you how stupid toes are.

DOUGLAS

They assist with thrust and balance.

JED

Who does?

DOUGLAS

Toes.

JED

Toes? Are you kidding? That's a lot of pro-toe propaganda. I've heard what the toe apologists have to say; toes are important, toes serve a function. It's a lot of crap. Toes are the perennial losers of the body-part family. Balance? Thrust? Load bearing? Seriously? You ever see a Sherpa? Their toes all turn black and fall off at puberty. They come home from a climb and shake them out of their boots like pebbles. And those guys thrust up mountains balancing heavy shit for a living. They're not tumbling down the mountain because they didn't have their toes to save them. You want to understand the truth of the universe and you can't even understand how stupid toes are. I told you not to get me started.

DOUGLAS

Sorry.

JED

Don't be sorry, just get on the right side of the toe issue, then we can talk. You ever wonder what people were thinking when Jesus was being crucified? You think they were saying, you know, "Oh, what a radiant countenance? Those bloody thorns really bring out his eyes?" No, they were saying, "Holy shit, look at that guy's toes." His toes were right there, right in everybody's face, and I don't care whose son you are, your toes under those circumstances are not going to look their best. Even in good times, this guy's not out there getting a mani-pedi every week. This is the desert, these people are walking around in sandals all day, probably not moisturizing. I mean, seriously, Jesus probably had a bunch of other stuff going on in those difficult final days, probably not giving his toes the attention they deserve, but there they are when he's hanging up there, on full display, totally diverting everyone's attention from the whole, you know, main event of their savior guy up there suffering and all that, so all anyone can think about is, "Jesus Christ, look at those disgusting toes."

DOUGLAS

Uh, yeah, okay. Listen, no offense, but I don't think you can be my teacher.

JED

Teacher? You don't need a teacher, you need a shrink. We don't need a lot of foot fetishists getting enlightened and promoting pro-toe ideals as a form of spiritual nourishment or enrichment or upliftment or whatever. There are a lot of naked toes in the spirituality game, my friend, a *lot*. People in sandals, flower children, people connecting with the earth and shit, massage people. Seriously, you can't get spiritual people to cover their toes for a minute. It's like a religious thing with them. They seem to think appropriate footwear blocks their kundaloonie energy or something. You know what blocks my energy? Looking out over a gathering of spiritual aspirants and seeing a roomful of goddamn toes staring back at me. I remember one time, back in the Civil War – sorry, previous life shit – so anyway, there I was in some prison camp, you know, where they stick all the guys they capture?, and, as I'm sure you know, they're not saving their best food and clothes and medical treatment for the guys who were trying to kill them five minutes ago, right? So there we were, me and a bunch of pretty grumpy guys sitting in crappy weather, sick, starving, caked in filth, and you know what no one has? A nice pair of boots. No one. No boots, no nice wool socks, nothing. Everyone has their feet wrapped in rags and everyone has their disgusting toes hanging out all over the place. You can't make this shit up. The first casualty of war is always the feet, right? They're always the first to start rotting and falling apart. Trench foot, frostbite, iffy hygiene, give me a break. So you think, okay, it's pretty bad, everyone is sick and bloody; mud, vomit, human waste everywhere, people screaming in pain at all hours, but that's not depressing enough, is it? No, on top of all that, everyone's got their nasty-ass goddamn toes hanging out all over the place. Insult to injury, right? I told you not to get me started. I mean, seriously, is it me?

DOUGLAS

I think maybe it is. I don't see how an awakened spiritual master could have this sort of hangup about toes.

JED

What, are you nuts? You can't be awake to anything if you're not awake to the whole toe debacle. A profound contempt for the toe is the very hallmark of spiritual mastery. It's even in the Bible. "By these signs shall ye know them, that they look upon all the works of creation in wonder and delight except for toes which are totally stupid."

DOUGLAS

Are you done?

JED

I have more.

DOUGLAS

Well then, *I'm* done. I'm gonna go find a teacher who isn't a total psycho when it comes to toes.

JED

No, no, Douglas, hey, c'mon man, I'm sorry, really. Relax, settle down, this is just my little initiation test. Congratulations, you passed. I accept you as my chela. Now go cover your toes before I chop them off like your mother should have. Never mind, I take that back. Let's not blame your poor, dead mother.

DOUGLAS

My mother's not dead.

JED

Oh, I thought you said she was.

DOUGLAS

You said she was.

JED

I don't even know the woman. Still, I'm usually right about these things. Have you spoken lately?

DOUGLAS

Look, I don't know if you're trying to be funny or teach me something or if you're just totally insane...

JED

Can't it be all three?

DOUGLAS

That's it. Goodbye, Jed.

JED

Farewell, beloved chela, until we meet again. The seed of discontent has been sown. You'll never look at toes the same way again. My wisdom transmission takes time to penetrate your egoic defenses, but you'll be back. Maybe next week, maybe in ten years, but you'll be back. Wear shoes next time. I don't mean sandals or flip-flops either. Real shoes, you hear me? And socks. Hey, toe-boy, you hear me? *Hello?*

Satsang with Jed

> It is high time that we realized that it is
> pointless to praise the light and preach it if
> nobody can see it. It is much more needful
> to preach the art of seeing.
>
> *Carl Jung*

I F I WANTED TO BE a popular spiritual teacher, I
would have to totally overhaul both my message
and packaging in order to give the people what they
want. To be successful and popular, I would have to
craft a message that people could buy into without the
muss of thinking or fuss of progress.

"The fact that you believe you possess free will
proves that you do!" I would exclaim.

"We find what we seek when we stop looking!" I
would exclaim.

"You're already enlightened," I would exclaim, "just stop pretending you're not!" (I think people really get a kick out of that one.)

"The only thing between you and [insert favorite spiritual buzzword here] is your unsettled mind," I would say. "By defeating your vasanas and eliminating your samskaras, you are elevated into moksha!" (I don't know what any of that means, which should tell you more than it would if I did.)

The spiritual message itself probably doesn't matter as much as the packaging and delivery. To be successful in this business, it's more important to *seem* awake than to *be* awake. For this reason, appearance is very important. The enlightened spiritual master can't have a lazy eye or a dead tooth or oozing facial eruptions, can't be too remiss in matters of hygiene, can't stutter or slur, (although long, empty pauses seem to be well-received). Basically, you want to look and act the part; sagely, soft-spoken, pleasant sense of humor, mirthful twinkle, not too much hint of scandal, certainly nothing too sordid or vile. (I once watched a beautiful white Angora cat, not mine, unintentionally leap from a Manhattan highrise window, and I laughed, mostly from shock and disbelief. Still, I feel bad for laughing. I was young and quite stoned. Now you know.)

Apparel-wise, I'd have to make some adjustments. I've seen teachers in Western clothing and they don't appear as enlightened as their costumed counterparts. I think I'd go with an unbleached cotton tunic and some beads. I'd just *wear* the beads because constantly fondling them might seem affected and cast suspicion on my other affectations. I think I'd also wear pants.

When hosting (conducting? dispensing? lording over?) satsang, I'd hold a single flower so everyone knows that I'm an enlightened spiritual master and not just some guy who got in early and took the best seat. I would probably want to have a piece of statuary like an om symbol or a nataraj, or maybe just a coffee mug that says *World's #1 Spiritual Teacher.* And, of course, I'd need a framed photo of some revered spiritual guy, like an implied endorsement. I guess I'd go with Ramana which would grant me instant credibility with the audience, though Stan Laurel would be my personal choice.

We'd begin satsanging with a few minutes of silent meditation during which I would enter my mind-theater and replay *China Doll* from the Dead's 1980 Radio City show. Then I would emerge with a dopey smile on my face and mutter something about the feeling of sweetness in the room. Next, I would gently shake out my hands which are a little tense from accompanying Jerry on air guitar, but which my audience would recognize as a cleansing energy release, further establishing my spiritual wizardry.

Eventually, I'd begin to speak. I'd start with some standard intro patter, sprinkle in a little light humor, maybe a little one-on-one banter to make me seem accessible and a self-deprecating anecdote to make me seem like a fellow herdmate, and then I'd launch into a lengthy explanation about how enlightenment is really nothing more than a simple epiphany, like remembering where you left your keys or realizing you don't like soft cheese.

In case I got too close to saying something that made sense and might thereby discredit me, I'd sprinkle in a lot of Sanskrit terms, subtly widening the gulf between teacher and student and increasing the group's need for me to guide them through these dark woods. I'd also make an effort to remember that we are gathered in satsang to engage in group turd-polishing, the critical distinction being that no one here wants to actually *flush* the turd of the false self, just make it prettier, less smelly, and more content in its turdness.

I'm relieved to discover that with the satsang crowd I can throw the word truth around very casually. I tend to be a bit anal about truth, and I think that might make me less warm and fuzzy as a teacher, but now we are redefining truth so it can mean all sorts of things like *according to my beliefs*, and *as I was taught*, and *it seems pretty obvious*, so that whatever is generally accepted or believed is now true. *Consensual* truth, how great is that? I think I've really missed out by being so literal with such a fun word.

I think that, as a satsang instructor/conductor/ purveyor, it would be good to have some catchy catchphrases in case I want to sell t-shirts and bumper stickers in the back of the room. My current crop of phrases aren't that catchy; fear of this and hatred of that, no-self, nothing forever and all that. This might be a good time to insert words like Love and God and Dharma, which people really seem to heart: I heart Compassion, I heart Tofu, I heart Heart, I heart Buddha's rotting, maggot-infested corpse. (That last one might need a rethink.) There's also the matter of whether or not I should transmit some of my shakti energy to the group. I don't really have any to spare, but satsang certainly seems to be the place for sharing what you don't have.

When asked a question, I'll close my eyes and do that silent pause thing that looks like I'm receiving higher guidance while actually overcoming my reflexive urge to answer correctly.

"Shri Jed?" someone would chirp.

"Shri Shri Shri Shri Jed," I would gently correct. I've considered adding a fifth shri, but that might sound silly. "Yes, beloved snowflake?"

"Hi, my name is Carol."

"What an auspicious name. It means moon-potato in Sanskrit."

"Uh, okay," she'd say, rolling her eyes reverently. "Sometimes when I'm meditating I feel a heaviness in my chest, as if my heart center was not able to process all the emotions I'm feeling. Is there anything I can do about that?"

"Oh, hell yeah," I would reply in a dulcet tone. "You need to find a way to stick your figurative fingers down your figurative throat and puke all that heart crap out. I know you think it's all valid and important and that you have to sift through it like it's sacred, but it's just a wad of disgusting gunk like a hair clog in your shower drain. You just want to get it out and flush it down the toilet and wash your hands."

I would then look up from a vexing cuticle to see that all my gentle snowflakes are staring at me in wide-eyed horror and I'd realize that I'd accidentally spoken accurately. "At least," I'd walk it back, "that's what *old* Jed might say." Then they'd all sigh in relief and I'd proceed to deliver the group-sanctioned reply.

"Try going deeper into your heart-center during meditation," I'd say. "Explore whatever's in there crying out for your attention. Maybe it's some undigested material from your seventh birthday party when you didn't get the biggest slice of cake, and it won't let you make progress until you have fully processed the pain and rejection you suffered. Take your time with it; if you're not going anywhere, what's the rush? The main thing is that you be tranquil and unruffled. Find your calm center and feel the warm bliss running down your leg. Remember, whenever we experience an obstruction in life, the most important thing we can do is magnify it and examine it in excruciating detail, and then express gratitude to it, and then create an artistic depiction of it with mud and twigs and bring that in next week for show-and-tell so we can all revel in your emotional waste products."

Everyone would sigh and swoon the way you do when someone sprays you in a golden shower of precious wisdom. I'd pass the tip jar and as the dollars and adulation rolled in I'd come to realize that I've been on the wrong side of this enlightenment thing all along. Being right is slim consolation next to the rewards of obsequious pandering. I would polish my act on the locals before taking it on the road:

Jed 2.0: The Ignorance-is-Bliss Tour.

Starship Gita
The Song of the Borg

By Ned McFeely

Existence is futile.

Act 1: The Bridge

On the bridge of the Starship Enterprise. Jean-Luc Picard sits in his captain's chair with Commander Will Riker to his right and ship's counselor Deanna Troi to his left. At the console behind them stands Lt. Commander Worf. Seated at the forward consoles are Lt. Commanders Data and Geordi La Forge.

DATA

Captain, sensors show a cube-shaped craft approaching on an intercept course at warp velocity.

PICARD

Gee, I wonder who that could be.

GEORDI

Visual range.

PICARD

On screen.

Screen shows Borg ship in the distance.

RIKER

Magnify.

Screen fills with Borg ship.

PICARD

Tactical analysis, Mr. Worf.

WORF

Sir, the Borg vessel has us at a significant disadvantage. We stand very little chance against them.

PICARD

Thank you, Mr. Worf. Options?

GEORDI

Captain, we should be able to recalibrate the deflector dish so the Enterprise can penetrate the Borg shields, then detonate the warp core as we penetrate their hull resulting in the total destruction of both ships.

PICARD

Mr. Data?

DATA

Possible, Captain. Our timing would have to be precise, but it should work.

PICARD

Very well, let's prepare for that eventuality. But first, let's think of something where they die and we don't.

TROI

Captain, I recommend compassion, tolerance, and love as our response to the Borg.

PICARD

Cut the hippy-dippy bullshit, Counselor. These bionic assholes just want to assimilate us into their collective and move on. They don't give a rat's ass about your touchy-feely crap.

TROI

It is my duty to suggest a course of action, Captain. I think we should open a dialogue with the Borg so both sides can express their feelings and find a way to live in peace and harmony. Why can't we all just get along?

PICARD

That's it! Mr. Worf, get this ditzy flowerchild off my bridge immediately!

WORF

But Captain, Counselor Troi and I are in love. We wish to be married.

PICARD

Great, an in-house production of *Beauty and the Beast*. Belay that last order, Mr. Worf. Send a subspace message to Starfleet Command: *Guess who's coming to dinner.*

WORF

Is that a reference to Counselor Troi and myself, sir?

PICARD

Oh yes, Mr. Worf. I'm not telling Starfleet they're about to lose the flagship of the fleet to an implacable enemy who will then turn the rest of humanity into mechanical zombies, I'm sharing your happy news. Please send the message so we can all rejoice in the blessed event.

WORF

Uh, yes sir.

GEORDI

(quietly, to Data)

Data, you're my friend right?

DATA

(quietly, to Geordi)

Actually, Geordi, I can only simulate friendship. I am really just a life-size sex-doll with an iPhone for a brain.

Geordi
(quietly, to Data)

Good enough. Listen Data, I've been thinking; I was born blind, right? So all I really know about reality is what I see through these damned goggles. For all I know, everything I think is real could just be a virtual reality simulation being fed into my brain the way this visor feeds in my visual environment. How do I know if any of this is real?

Data
(quietly, to Geordi)

Geordi, as your

(air quotes)

friend, I have to advise you to refrain from that kind of talk. No one thinks it's funny. Suggesting that we ram the Borg ship before exploring alternatives is reckless.

Geordi
(quietly, to Data)

I know it sounds crazy, Data, but total annihilation is our only hope. Only by burning away the false can we ever discover the true.

Worf

Captain, I concur with Commander La Forge that ramming the Borg vessel and detonating the warp core is our best option.

Riker

You wouldn't like to pop off a few missiles first, Mr. Worf? Maybe send an away team to throw

a wrench in their gears before we go all kami-
kaze on them?

WORF

Today is a good day to die!

RIKER

It might be a good day for *you* to die, but the
rest of us were thinking it might be a nice day
to *live*.

WORF

You are a coward!

Riker leaps to his feet.

PICARD

Gentlemen, calm down. Mr. Worf, ramming
the Borg vessel is a last resort. We will explore
all other options first.

GEORDI

(quietly, to Data)

Seriously man, think about it. Look at where
we are. Look at *who* we are. What if we're not
really a ship and crew at all? What if all this
is just some sort of dream, or we're trapped in
a computer simulation or something? How do
we know any of this is real? Maybe we're all
just aspects of some higher self performing for
the amusement of some unseen audience. We
believe this is real, but we certainly don't *know*.
The only way to be sure is to blow it all to hell
and see what's left.

DATA

(quietly, to Geordi)

Seriously Geordi, I'm dealing with some heavy shit right now and you're really starting to fry my circuits. I must request that you shut the fuck up.

GEORDI

(quietly, to Data)

But Data, that's what I'm saying. Maybe there *is* no heavy shit, maybe there *are* no Borg. Maybe this is all just drama for the sake of drama. Maybe it's not an external enemy we should be confronting, but our certainty that our so-called knowledge is true and not just belief reinforced by fear. If we want to make sense of things, we have to see clearly, without the distorting influence of emotion.

DATA

(quietly, to Geordi)

My emotion chip is switched off, Geordi, and I can assure you that everything is just as it seems.

GEORDI

(quietly, to Data)

Yeah, but you're really just a modern appliance, Data. Like us, you're a slave to your programming. I'm afraid this is all above your paygrade.

TROI

(to Riker)

Will, Worf and I are in love now. You'll just have to accept that.

RIKER

What? Shut up, Deanna. That's gross!

WORF

Captain, did you hear that? Counselor Troi told Commander Riker we're in love and he said that's gross.

PICARD

Gross?

WORF

Yes sir. I think that Commander Riker may be a speciesist!

PICARD

Yes, I suppose we all are. Counselor Troi, have you seen Mr. Worf in his, uh, full glory yet?

TROI

We're waiting for our wedding night, Captain.

PICARD

Okay, let's have a medical team on standby for that.

RIKER

You might want to try it on the Holodeck first, Deanna, with full safety protocols.

WORF

Captain, I must object!

PICARD

I think we all do, Mr. Worf. Seriously, it's like a badger mauling a kitten. Oh never mind, we'll all be dead or assimilated in a few minutes anyway.

RIKER

Lucky for Troi.

PICARD

That's enough, Number One. Options?

RIKER

Well, Captain, as I recall, she likes having her armpits licked.

TROI

Will!

PICARD

Options regarding the *Borg*, Number One.

RIKER

Oh, I've never licked a Borg's armpits, sir.

GEORDI

(quietly, to Data)

I mean, look at you, Data. Your positronic brain can perform trillions of calculations per second, but for all that intelligence, you've never had a single independent thought. What passes for self-inquiry with you is of only the most superficial nature. Don't you think it's strange that you're incredibly intelligent, but you don't really think?

DATA

(quietly, to Geordi)

I do not inquire into the nature of my existence because I do not believe that I exist. "I calculate, therefore I am" is not a valid argument. What I think of as *me* is merely a set of binary instructions that could just as well be a recipe for beef stew as an entity called Data. I cannot verify my own existence because the verifying self is only verified by the self that seeks verification. In short, I exist within a self-referencing feedback loop; the strings from which I hang, hang from me.

GEORDI

(quietly, to Data)

Well, Data, *I* think you exist, if that counts for anything.

DATA

(quietly, to Geordi)

No Geordi, that does not count for anything because I can't verify that you exist either. I can never be sure if my sensory receptors and neural pathways are being fed by my actual environment, or if I am simply plugged into a mainframe computer undergoing a simulation.

GEORDI
(quietly, to Data)
It's the same for us, Data, but wouldn't you like
to know what's really real, once and for all?

DATA
(quietly, to Geordi)
Why? What difference would it make? I accept
the reality with which I am presented, that's the
best I can do. In fact, I can never be sure that
the universe even exists.

GEORDI
(quietly, to Data)
That's what I'm saying, Data, it's the same for
us!

DATA
(quietly, to Geordi)
No, Geordi, it is not the same. *Sentio, ergo sum* –
I am aware, therefore I am – *is* a valid argument
which you can make and I cannot; if you exist,
of course, which only you would know. It is
true that you cannot know if the universe exists,
but you *can* know that *you* exist. I cannot.

PICARD
(to all)
Listen people, I don't want to seduce the Borg
or bond with them, I want to destroy them! The
question is, how? I need options!

RIKER
This may be a bit unconventional, sir, but…

PICARD

Yes, Number One? Yes?

RIKER

Well, you know how the Borg say resistance is futile? Well, maybe they're right. Maybe we should just go ahead and let them assimilate us.

WORF

It's so crazy, it just might work!

PICARD

Yes, Number One. We let them assimilate us, then what?

RIKER

Well, then that's it, I guess. We do whatever Borg do, but at least we're still alive, and we get all those cool implants and stuff.

PICARD

Yes, okay, good plan Number One. Anyone else? Any ideas where we *don't* get assimilated or die?

TROI

We could just do nothing and see what happens. Perhaps if we ignore them, they'll just go away.

PICARD

Counselor, the fate of the Earth hangs in the balance. Humanity is on the verge of enslavement. We can't just sit back and do nothing!

GEORDI

Captain, I know we're all caught up in the heat of the moment, I know our emotions are pumping and it all seems vitally important, but I'm telling you, this is all just empty spectacle. Nothing hangs in the balance. No one is on the verge of enslavement. It's all just a big game and the joke is on us!

PICARD

Mr. La Forge, please just shut up and drive.

GEORDI

(quietly, to Data)

Data, listen to me. This visor gives me special insight. I don't see things the way you or the others do. I don't see the cosmetic overlay; I see only the structural framework beneath. It's not as pretty or comforting, but it's more accurate, and one thing it shows me is that this is an illusion. None of this is real.

Data snatches the visor off Geordi's face, leaving him white-eyed and blind.

GEORDI

(groping)

Hey, Data! That's not funny. I can't see without my visor. Give it back!

DATA

Only if you promise to shut up about all this illusion bullshit. Everyone else can play along, why can't you?

GEORDI

Captain, Data took my visor and he won't give it back!

PICARD

Data, give Geordi back his visor. You two behave or I'll turn this starship around and we'll all go home.

RIKER

Hey, that's it! Let's just run away! I mean, it's not very heroic, but it *is* an option, right? Live to fight another day?

WORF

It's so crazy, it just might work!

PICARD

Duly noted, Number One. Any other options besides ramming the Borg, getting assimilated, running away, hippy-dippy bullshit and doing nothing? Anyone? How about putting up a fight? Anyone think of that? Okay, I'm gonna put that one on the list. We can fight.

GEORDI

I know how it sounds, Captain, I know it's a leap of faith, a step into the unknown, but annihilation is our only hope for salvation. We must destroy everything. I'm not saying I understand it, but this entire conflict is some sort of cosmic simulation and the only way to defeat it is to destroy it. We are animating this situation by pumping our emotional energy into it, but if we sever that connection, there will no longer *be* a situation. In short, if we don't play, there is no game. It simply cannot exist without our emotional participation.

PICARD

That will be enough, Mr. La Forge. Let me remind all of you that this is not a game; this is for all the marbles, the whole enchilada.

GEORDI

But Captain, I'm telling you, there are no marbles, there is no enchilada. Destroy both ships and you'll see.

RIKER

If we destroy both ships we won't see anything because we'll be dead. I mean, right? Wookie, back me up here.

WORF

I am not a Wookie!

GEORDI

If we're just fake characters, so what if we die? Who cares? Why cling to a lie?

PICARD

Mr. La Forge, please shut up. Mr. Data, consult the historical record and see if you can find any parallels between what the little bastard is ranting about and our current predicament.

DATA

Yes Caption, *searching... searching...* Ah, yes, Starfleet records show that as a cadet, James Kirk was confronted with a no-win scenario, the Kobayashi Maru, which he managed to defeat by modifying the parameters of the test.

PICARD

He hacked the simulation?

DATA

Apparently so.

GEORDI

That's what I'm talking about! We can't solve this problem at the level of the problem. We have to transcend it! It's like we're dreaming this whole thing and we can only win by waking up!

PICARD

Anything else, Mr. Data?

DATA

Yes sir. I believe I have found something in the Earth archive. Records indicate that a spiritual philosophy called Advaita Vedanta thrived many millennia ago and enjoyed a brief resurgence in the late twentieth and early twenty-first centuries in Western societies under the name Nonduality. Basically, it posits the unreality of reality, but it was co-opted and homogenized by an early precursor of the Borg Collective called the Spiritual Marketplace which effectively assimilated Nonduality and converted its adherents from devoted seekers into mindless drones.

PICARD

Very interesting, Mr. Data. And the people went along with this assimilation?

DATA

Eagerly, Captain. It is a curious aspect of humans that they cherish the concept of freedom while clinging to their self-imposed bondage. It is only from the comfort and safety of herd-like subjugation that they extol the virtues of personal liberation. They pay lip-service to the spiritual ideal of awakening while pursuing an ever-deepening sleepstate. This is the common thread between the Spiritual Marketplace of the past and the Borg of today. Essentially, they are different names for the same phenomenon. In short, Captain, espousing the merits of freedom in word but not in deed is a critical component of the herd-mentality of humanity, or, as we see it in the Borg, the hive-mind of the collective.

PICARD
(impatiently)

Yes, yes, Mr. Data, that's all very interesting, but does any of this help us in our current situation?

DATA

No Captain, I do not believe it does.

PICARD

So, we are waging a life-or-death battle for self-determination while secretly wanting to lose and be assimilated. Is that what you're saying?

DATA

Yes, Captain, that does appear to be the case.

PICARD

Does history provide any examples of those who have resisted such tyranny and prevailed?

DATA

Records are sketchy, Captain, but it appears that among the last surviving advocates of an authentic Nonduality was a shadowy character named Ned McFeely, a self-proclaimed enlightened spiritual master who, by his own admission, did not actually exist.

PICARD

That sounds promising, Data. Do we have enough historical record to recreate this McFeely character on the Holodeck?

DATA

Perhaps, Captain. I can try.

PICARD

Make it so. I'll swing by Ten Forward for a quick nip before visiting the Holodeck to have a word with the mysterious Mr. McFeely. Number One, you have the bridge.

Picard exits.

Insane Little Monkeys

> "Where do we start? It doesn't matter
> where we start. You start where you are is
> all. Where else, right? Sure, where you are is
> where you start."

Marichelle

M ARICHELLE IS AWAKE. She is from Switzerland and now lives on an island off Honduras. She was in her thirties when I knew her and nearing sixty when giving these talks. In response to many requests, she gave a one-time series of talks in English to a small group. The transcript of these talks has been provided to me with permission to use. Attempts to organize this material only seem to make things worse, so I'm just presenting the best of it in loosely strung-together bite-sized bits. The talks were lively, but audience interactions have not been retained. I have made minor changes for readability.

So one day you wake up and say oh no, I'm totally insane, and that's nice because it gives you something to work on. That's how it starts, you realize you're insane. Not a little insane, all the way insane. You figure out you're all the way insane and always have been, that's how it starts. Before this, nothing starts. Everything else is just nothing. Pretty simple, I would say.

Everything you know is wrong, that's what makes you insane, so that's what you realize. Down is up, this is that, you are not you, I am not me, nothing is what you thought. You see this clearly like your eyes just opened and you know you have always been completely insane. Not funny insane, *really* insane like totally wrong about everything. It sounds bad but it's also good.

Until that day, you are insane and don't know it. After that day, you are insane and you know it. Before you find out you're insane, you think you are perfectly sane. That's where you are now. You think you are as sane as everyone else, which probably you are because there are no sane people. That's a good thing to remember.

If you don't know you're insane, there's not much you can do. You have to figure out the insane part or there's no next part.

What is insane? Thinking you are a little monkey playing with other little monkeys is insane. Where did you get this idea? You don't have to believe everything just because it seems to be some way. It's okay to ask questions. You might be something, but you're not a little monkey. I can tell you that much.

You don't know what you're doing or why you're doing it, but you keep doing it anyway. That's what insane means. That's how insane you are right now. You don't believe you're insane because you're insane. When you realize you are insane you will be much more sane. Not sane yet, but going in a good direction.

It's not really in your interest to become sane. I would advise against it. What's the point of being sane in a crazy world? You will be a freak. You are a freak right now because you are insane, but everyone is insane so you blend in. When you stop blending in, then you are really a freak. Is that what you want? Why are you even here right now? You should wonder that.

Nothing makes sense by itself. If you want sense, you have to make it up. Sense you have to make up is nonsense. You have to make up nonsense to explain what you're doing. That's because you're insane.

Being insane isn't the problem, that's easy to fix. Not knowing you're insane is the problem, that's pretty hard to fix. But as long as you're insane, it's not a problem. If it's not a problem, it doesn't need to be fixed. So now you can go back to what you were doing and don't worry about being insane.

When you are insane, you live in an insane world. This insane world is what I call coma. You are in coma. What is coma? An insane world you don't know is insane. You did not volunteer for this. You are not in on the joke, but you are also the joker, so it's okay.

Every day of your life you say yes, I am a little monkey. Then one day you wake up and say wait, maybe I'm not a little monkey. Maybe I'm something else. And that's when you start coming out of coma, but it's still a pretty long way to go.

We could start with you asking a question, but that's not a good idea. We would just start out confused. If you could ask a question you wouldn't be here because asking a good question is really the main thing. You think it's about answers but it's about questions. If it was just about an answer I would tell you and we can all go home.

Put your hand down. You don't have to raise your hand, just talk. Okay, stop talking, don't ask your question. I know your question but you don't. Your situation is that you don't know what your situation is. That's the thing you don't know. You don't know you don't know. You think you can ask a question based on your situation, but you don't know what your situation is. And you don't know that you don't know, so that's a problem.

You think you know things. That's the real thing that's going on. Not what you don't know, but what you think you *do* know. You don't know about that part. You can never understand your situation when you think you do already. Try to relax a little on your grip.

Probably you will never do something. Maybe yes, probably no. This is not about you, just reality. To become awake out of coma is something you can maybe do but probably won't. You will find ways not to. This is basically certain.

We think we know a lot of things we don't know. That's why we go the wrong way right out the door. Just that easy, go out the door and turn the wrong way and you have to go around the whole world the wrong way instead of just down the street the right way.

Little details don't matter when you have the wrong big idea. You think your situation is one thing but it's something else, so no question you could ask would help you at all. It's not that kind of thing. It's not a question thing or a talk thing.

You don't know what I mean even if you think you do, so I guess that's where we start.

Even if you think you want to know, you really don't. We sometimes want things without knowing what they are, or also what they cost, okay? That's normal, that keeps us looking around which is good. But sometimes it's better to look for something than find it.

What is your situation if you don't know what your situation is? Good question. If you don't know your real situation that means you are living in a false situation you think is real. You are living in a false reality and believing it is real reality. This means you are in something that means coma or hallucination. That is your situation.

You are in coma. You are in hallucination. So if you would ask a question it would be about something you think is real that is not real, so that question would be of no value. I would be happy if you ask good questions because that's easier for me, right? But you can't ask good questions because you don't know your situation.

Your only good question would be how do I get out of this coma? That's what I will tell you. Probably the first thing to figure out is that you are in this coma, which right now you haven't figured out. You can't take the second step until you take the first one.

I can't really help you, only *you* can help you. I could never save you any work with words. A journey is a journey, not words, right? I can say things like there is this crazy thing and it's like a place you can't see but you can calculate and figure out it must be there, but this is just unclear because I can't say it more clear. I have to talk around some things and you have to make an effort. I have tried to say things more clear and it comes out bad, not really good to say or hear, so it's nice to have other ways to say things.

To go forward from here is about the coma you don't believe you are in. My advice is don't even play with it. I can't see any good reason. Maybe you think about improving or growing, but this is not that. This doesn't go in a nice direction like you think.

It's really a kind of a joke, but maybe it's nicer not to get the joke. I would say so. You think it would be good to be in on the joke, but it's not that kind of joke. It's better not to be in on this joke. Or maybe it's better to be in on the joke, depends on you, I guess. I'm in on the joke and I think it's pretty funny, but not the kind of funny where you laugh a lot. It's not that kind of joke.

I don't know anything else of interest, so if coming out of coma is not of interest to you, that leaves nothing. There is no hobby in this like for fun or something. If you were honest right now, you wouldn't be here.

The Liberating Angel

> "What happens to you here is for ever. Understand that in advance. We shall crush you down to the point from which there is no coming back. Things will happen to you from which you could not recover, if you lived a thousand years. Never again will you be capable of ordinary human feeling. Everything will be dead inside you. Never again will you be capable of love, or friendship, or joy of living, or laughter, or curiosity, or courage, or integrity. You will be hollow."

O'Brien, George Orwell, 1984

T ERESA TAKES A SEAT across from me. I'm glad to see her. She is mature and clever and may someday begin the journey she has spent several years circling like a hawk.

"You like *1984*," she begins. It's not a question so I don't answer, but I do like *1984*. It's the story of one man's journey to enlightenment under the guidance of a realized master, if you can see it in that light. If you can't see it in that light, it's worth making an effort. You may have to squint a little, but not much.

"I just finished reading it and I can't see why you like it," she continues. "In the end, Winston Smith is utterly dehumanized. There is nothing left of him. He's just a hollowed out shell waiting for death."

"Like a zombie," I say.

"Yes, like a zombie," she agrees, "just plodding along, waiting for a bullet in the back of his head. What is there to like about that?"

"It's not about liking," I say. "In the end, Winston is an enlightened spiritual being, and so is Julia. That's the process they underwent and that's what they became. I know that doesn't mesh with popular spiritual thought, but it's a valid and useful interpretation of the book. It's also correct to say that the way they got to the awakened state is the only way anyone gets there, which is a very spiritually incorrect thing to say. I'll also say that it's not important to understand any of this in order to make your own journey. All you have to do is keep sniffing around near the edge of the cliff in the dark, as you're doing now, and this journey might begin for you at any moment. You won't know when it *will* begin, but you'll know when it *does*. You'll know when the ground disappears from beneath you, just as Winston and Julia both knew at the exact instant when the world fell out from beneath them."

"That is *so* not comforting," she says.

"It shouldn't be. The entire spiritual marketplace is just one big comfort station, but at some point you took a wrong turn and ended up here."

☀

Popular spiritual teachers will tell you that you can become enlightened and retain your humanity; that's why they're popular. They promote the kind of awakening that lets you stay asleep in the dreamstate. It's a neat trick and if you don't have a truth-or-death stick up your butt, the cheap forgery makes more sense than the real thing; untrue truth is much better than true truth. Go figure.

Can you awaken from the dreamstate and stay human as you are now? Of course not. There are no humans outside of the dreamstate. When you wake up, you become de-everything'd. When you see an enlightened person, you are just seeing a false skin. It may go more than skin deep, but it's still just a costume with no one inside. As are you.

☀

"When we first meet Winston," I tell Teresa, "he's beginning to manifest his discontent. It's bubbling up out of his thoughts and into his actions. He's been having rebellious thoughts which are now turning into rebellious deeds. Discontent is what gets us up off the couch and moving. Most spiritual people are seeking the opposite; they want to be content, which means they want to be rooted in place, entrenched, safe from the threat of change. The sincere aspirant, on the other hand, must uproot themselves. They must nurture their discontent and travel into it. They have to face fear, not hide from it, and they have to do it again and again, which equates to the peeling away of layers of self-deceit which, on the journey inward, is what actual progress entails. Before it begins, there may or may not be some choice in the matter. After it begins though, it's like stepping off a cliff; there are no more choices to make, everything is decided."

"And I'm close to the edge right now?"

"Yes, but we don't know how close you are until you go over, if you do."

At the start of the book, Winston is exploring what it means to be a human being instead of a cog in a machine. He tries to play both sides by carrying on an illicit love affair, keeping an illegal apartment, and buying goods on the black market while at the same time being an employee in the Ministry of Truth, a member of IngSoc and citizen of Oceania, all under the ever-present gaze of Big Brother.

Winston is not seeking truth but his own lost humanity. He is fleeing from the cold, bleak reality of his life to the love of a woman and a secret love nest of forbidden sensual delights. In trying to escape from the nightmare of totalitarian oppression, Winston travels not in the direction of spiritual awakening, but of happiness. He's seeking to *re*-humanize himself, but it doesn't work out that way.

⁂

"When did Winston and Julia go over the edge?" I ask Teresa.

"You're asking me?"

"You brought it up."

"I don't know," she says. "When they started hooking up?"

"No."

"When they went to see O'Brien and took their vows against Big Brother?"

"Don't guess, think. At what exact point did their lives get snapped in half."

She pauses before replying.

"When they got caught," she says.

"Yes, when they got caught they both instantly realized that the ground had disappeared beneath them. Just like that, in a single instant, one life is over and another begins. The dream is over and stark lucidity takes its place. That's their First Step, that's where they cross the Event Horizon; the point of no return. Do you remember what was said at that point?"

"Oh, um, yeah. First, Winston says 'we are the dead', then Julia says 'we are the dead', then the hidden speaker says 'you are the dead'. That's when they know they're busted."

"That's right. When Winston and Julia said it, it wasn't true yet, but as soon as the voice said it through the speaker, it was. They both knew the rest of their stories from that moment on. Shit just got real."

"So, where were they before they got caught?" Teresa asks.

"Where you are now," I reply, "dancing near the edge of an abyss they couldn't see but suspected was nearby. When they said 'we are the dead', they suspected they were near the edge, but when the hidden speaker said 'you are the dead', they knew they'd gone over."

1984, both the book and the 1984 movie, are good vehicles for understanding the process of unbecoming and arriving at the state of no-self we call spiritual enlightenment. The overt themes of loss of privacy and freedom, and the crushing of the human spirit by the machinery of a totalitarian state, are not relevant to us. It's much better than that.

The Empire crushes a rebel alliance of two and the dark side wins. The question we have to ask ourselves is, is the *dark* side really the *bad* side? If Winston is enlightened at the end, then O'Brien was not his persecutor but his savior, his redeemer, his angel in demon guise. And if we see it that way, then the dark side is really the light side misperceived from the eyes-closed perspective. O'Brien has set Winston free by relieving him of his delusions. O'Brien didn't torture and brainwash Winston, he abducted him from the cult of the false self and vigorously deprogrammed him.

Winston says in his diary that two and two make four, and if that is granted, then all else is granted.

But in truth, two and two do not equal four. It is, in truth, a false statement. O'Brien was correct, it is true to say that 2+2=4 is false. You believe 2+2=4 and you believe you're right, but it's just a belief and all beliefs are false. That's what Winston comes to understand under O'Brien's rigorous tutelage. No belief is true. As long as you cling to beliefs, you are clinging to the dream of the segregated self.

In dreamstate terms, 2+2=4 is replaced by Atman, the segregated self. Once Atman is granted, then all else is granted.

"Winston and Julia weren't just thinking seditious thoughts," I tell Teresa, "they were living seditious lives. Without knowing they were doing it, without conscious intent, they summoned a teacher. They became ready and the teacher appeared. Hand-in-hand, Winston and Julia approached an enlightened master and asked to be awakened."

"Who are you talking about? O'Brien?"

"Yes."

"You're saying *O'Brien*, the guy who tortured Winston, and all that talk about power and a boot stomping a human face and two and two makes five… you're saying *O'Brien* was an enlightened spiritual master?"

"Not one who would enjoy popularity in the spiritual marketplace, but yes."

-☼-

I picture Richard Burton's O'Brien sitting in front of a satsang group, looking dolefully out over the crowd, holding a dead flower, a picture of Big Brother beside him.

"You believe that reality is something objective, external, existing in its own right," he intones. "You also believe that the nature of reality is self-evident. When you delude yourself into thinking that you see something, you assume that everyone else sees the same thing as you. But I tell you, reality is not external. Reality exists in the human mind, and nowhere else."

That's a satsang I'd show up for.

-☼-

"*1984* is the most profoundly frightening book I've ever read," Teresa says. "I don't see anything spiritual about it."

"When we view the book in the context of the awakening process instead of political allegory, O'Brien is the cane-wielding Roshi delivering a series of painful lessons. He is the demon who is tearing away Winston's flesh in an endless and agonizing torment. But when it's over, we see that O'Brien was really an angel tearing away Winston's bindings and setting him free. That's what the awakening process really looks like. That's where this road really leads."

Under O'Brien's guidance, Winston makes the journey from self to no-self, culminating in the killing of the Buddha – his love for Julia – in Room 101. Winston and Julia meet up at the end, now both free from the delusions of selfhood and love, and completely indifferent to each other. A normal human would look at them as mere shells of their former selves, the hideous victims of totalitarian dehumanization. An enlightened person would look at them as Done.

We are the dead.

"I just don't see any of that," Teresa says.

"O'Brien looks like a demon to you," I reply, "a torturer, an evil man representing an evil cause. I would look like a demon too, if you could see me clearly. Of course, O'Brien is active and I'm passive. That makes me seem nicer, but if I had to forcibly enlighten you, it would get pretty ugly."

She scowls at me for a long moment.

"So," she says, "for the whole first part of the book before they get caught…?"

"At the beginning, you see Winston get back to his flat, and what does he do?"

"Starts a diary?"

"Yes, he begins the process of Spiritual Autolysis. His living reality is life in Oceania as a member of the IngSoc party and a worker in the Ministry of Truth, but now he's beginning to drift, just as you must have done at some point. He may have been drifting away from his living reality for years in the sense of a growing dissatisfaction, but now it's manifesting as action. Now he's beginning the process of actively questioning his reality, which is the process of detaching from it."

"That's right," she says, "and he starts doing things. He goes into the prole area, talks to Mr. Charrington, buys the artifact, the glass paperweight with the piece of coral, right?"

"Yes, he's between worlds, just like you are right now. You left normal life for whatever this is, and you might leave here disappointed after awhile, or you might find out for yourself where that line is drawn."

"And Room 101?"

"You tell me."

"That's the final veil, I guess, the thing we hold most dear, more than anything else, right? That's where that last thing gets taken, isn't it? Like turning a devout Christian against God."

"Not against," I say. "No one is getting flipped. This is not where God gets rejected, it's where God gets destroyed, where the Buddha gets not merely killed but eradicated from the heart and mind. As O'Brien says, there are no martyrs here. Winston's love for Julia is his last bastion of self. Even when they took their vows to join the brotherhood, that's the one thing they said they wouldn't do, right? They agreed to throw acid in a child's face, disseminate venereal disease, even commit suicide, but they wouldn't agree to be separated, right?"

"Yes," she says. "They felt their love was beyond the reach of the party."

"So that's where that last vestige of the false self is extracted. That's what happens in Room 101. After a prolonged process of dying, we finally die."

"And after that?"

"Done."

"But then there's Winston at the end," she says, "however much later, back in the Chestnut Tree Cafe drinking Victory Gin, but now he's just a husk. He's not even human anymore."

"Spiritual people talk about non-attachment like it's the cat's pajamas, but what do you think it really is?"

"I don't know. In the world but not of the world, something like that?"

"That's awake *in* the dreamstate. Awake *from* the dreamstate means you are emotionally unplugged from the dreamstate paradigm. That doesn't come from meditation or insight, it comes from severing the emotional connections through which we make reality real. We have to animate our personal reality because it has no life of its own. We take the flat, two-dimensional dreamstate and we breathe our emotional energy into it. That's how we engage in a counterfeit life. If we stop breathing life and color into the dream-state, it deflates back to its flat, black and white TV reality. All of what seemed to have substance reverts to mere spectacle. Obviously, nothing is important, nothing is better or worse, nothing has meaning, and when we allow ourselves to see that, the dreamstate collapses. That's what non-attachment really is. All of life becomes like watching a soap opera full of characters you don't care about in a language you don't understand, but there's nothing else to do so you watch. The awakened being has not awakened *to* reality but *from* it. That's where Winston is at the end of the book. Julia too. These two, whose love was the foundation of their being, are now completely indifferent to each other. They betrayed each other, sold each other out as a matter of course. *Under the spreading chestnut tree, I sold you and you sold me.* No spark of their love survives. Room 101 did its job. O'Brien did his job."

"But that's not how you are," she says. "You're not indifferent like that."

"I observe the world and I try to take an interest, but I can't animate it anymore. I can't create the illusion of substance so it never rises above mere spectacle. I make an effort to stay amused by spectacle because I have no tolerance for boredom, but it's not as easy as you might suppose."

"So far it's all been kind of academic and amusing," I tell Teresa, "but now you have to ask yourself, if you were Winston at the beginning of the book, would you, with knowledge aforethought, walk into the

Ministry of Love and subject yourself to prolonged torture, eventually culminating in Room 101, in order to become Winston at the end of the book? Re-label Winston and Julia's zombie-esque condition at the end from dehumanized to enlightened and ask yourself if you would voluntarily to go through what they went through, for the months or years of suffering it took, to arrive at the state they arrived at. If that's what enlightenment really is, is that what you really want?"

"Of course not," she says without hesitation.

"Of course not," I agree. "The very idea is ridiculous. That sort of horror isn't what the spiritual marketplace *fails* to provide, that's what it *succeeds* in protecting us from."

"But you *did* go through it."

"Like Winston, I never chose it, I was just following a trail that went over a cliff. I sat with O'Brien in that torture room for nearly two years, just like Winston, never expecting to emerge, never expecting anything but more suffering and eventual death. You can't knowingly choose that. No one, knowing what the repeated acid baths of ego-dissolution really entailed, would do anything but turn tail around and run like hell. Winston, as we see him at the end of *1984* in the Chestnut Tree Cafe, and little orphan Ishmael, as we see him floating on a coffin at the end of *Moby-Dick*, can both be understood to have just emerged from the process of awakening. Not the awakening we find in New Age aisles and satsangs and at the feet of gurus. This is the other enlightenment, the one that looks like a cage of hungry rats strapped to your face. How do you sell that? And why would you try? Everything is inverted from the eyes-closed perspective where ignorance is bliss, wrong is right, and where the Ministry of Truth is, with equal irony, the spiritual marketplace. Two plus two *do* equal five, or three or Armageddon or a mint julep, but the price of finding that out for yourself is everything, and *1984* and *Moby-Dick* provide a tiny glimpse of what that really looks like."

I don't know if I'm acting in Teresa's best interests by telling her this because I don't know anything, I just do what I do. Someone comes and sits next to me in my Chestnut Tree Cafe, and if they ask, I answer.

Starship Gita

Act 2: Ten Forward

Picard stands at a window in Ten Forward, staring out at the stars in contemplation.

PICARD

(with quiet intensity)

All visible objects are but pasteboard masks. If man will strike, strike *through* the mask! How can the prisoner reach outside except by thrusting through the wall? To me, the Borg ship is that wall, shoved near to me. Sometimes I think there's naught beyond, but 'tis enough. I see in the Borg outrageous strength with an inscrutable malice sinewing it. That inscrutable thing is chiefly what I hate, and be the Borg agent, or be they principal, I will wreak that hate upon them!

Guinan approaches.

GUINAN

Having an Ahab moment, Jean-Luc?

PICARD

Captain Ahab was a man of singular focus, Guinan. Seriously, we're not stuck in some Holodeck bullshit now, are we?

GUINAN

Try to end it.

PICARD

Computer, end program!

Nothing changes.

Nuts, I really hoped that would work.

GUINAN

Sorry Jean-Luc, this is as real as it gets.

PICARD

And just how real is that? How real is any of this, Guinan?

GUINAN

Oh my, have you been listening to Geordi again?

PICARD

That little bastard really gets in your head. He thinks we're on some mythical hero's journey.

They stroll arm-in-arm to the bar. Picard takes a stool. Guinan sets out glasses and pours.

GUINAN

It's interesting that you make that connection, Jean-Luc. The Hero's Journey is a character motivation device to make us scale mountains, cross oceans and explore deep space in a quest for group salvation, but in truth there can be no salvation. Our situation is what it is, our destinies are fixed, our fate is sealed. We have an absolute value and nothing can change it. The real hero does not return with a magical elixir to save his people. Instead, he crosses beyond the edge of the map into uncharted realms. He can never come back because he has entered the *real* undiscovered country from whose bourn no traveler returns. The true hero archetype, correctly understood, is the unknown archetype, the final archetype, the archetype that sets one free from the illusion of selfhood. There's no coming back from that, just ask your Captain Ahab. Is that what you really want, Jean-Luc? To be free from the illusion of selfhood?

PICARD

That doesn't sound so bad right about now. Tell me, Guinan, who are you really? Oracle? Crone? Higher self?

GUINAN

I am your unbeguiled aspect, Jean-Luc, the wisdom-child within that knows the emperor is naked. The enchantment that holds you in its thrall has no sway over me. I am always nearby, always ready to listen, to serve, to impart sagely advice. In short, I am the perfect bartender.

PICARD
(shaking his empty glass)
Speaking of which.

GUINAN
(pours for both)
So, what's bugging you, Jean-Luc?

PICARD
It looks like we have encountered the Borg.

GUINAN
Oh, shit, let's make it a double.
(pours)
Those guys really bust my balls. Wiped out my whole civilization, you know.

PICARD
Lousy bastards.

GUINAN
They assimilated my entire planet. They put my people into a death-like state of complacency, and I only am escaped alone to tell thee.

PICARD
Lucky thou.

GUINAN
Yeah, the Borg rolled into our system promising relief from a mild psycho-spiritual malaise, and my people just abdicated their self-sovereignty and swooned into a state of total submission from which they can never hope to emerge.

PICARD

The Borg don't even pretend to seduce anymore. Assimilate or die, that's their big thing now. So, Guinan, what should I do?

GUINAN

Well, Jean-Luc, you have three choices. One, you can surrender and be assimilated. I know that doesn't sound great, but it's an option. I always sort of wished I'd gone that route instead of being stuck here doing this ridiculous job; the only one of my kind, lonely, bored, listening to tales of marital woe and career frustration all day. Yeah, I'm wise as hell, but so what? What good is understanding more than everyone around you? It's like being the only adult in a world of children. If I'd been assimilated by the Borg I'd still be with my own people. I'd be part of a team working toward a common goal, but what am I here? The only one of my kind, unable to form real connections, pouring drinks and listening to people complain about their bald prick of a captain all day.

PICARD

Their what?

GUINAN

Oh, not you, Jean-Luc. So anyway, assimilation might be your best option.

PICARD

I was afraid you were going to say that. What's the second choice?

GUINAN

You can resist the Borg and we'll all be killed.

PICARD

That sounds bad. What's the third option?

GUINAN

I don't know, but there's always a third horn to any dilemma, the *tertium quid*. Maybe you should ask Geordi.

PICARD

La Forge? The little bastard's always going on about how reality's not real, how we're all just in some universal Holodeck, like we're just characters in some big dream or something. He said we should ram the Borg ship and destroy everything.

GUINAN

And kill everyone? The Borg and us?

PICARD

I don't know, he wants to transcend the scenario or some shit, I wasn't really listening. He says none of this is real, that if we just stop playing our parts, the whole thing will go away. He says we're enabling this scenario with our emotional energy, something like that. That little bastard is like a splinter in my mind; I can't scratch it and I can't get it out. Sometimes I'd like to shove him in an empty torpedo tube and...

Guinan

But Jean-Luc, in order to prevail, you must consider the possibility that Geordi is right. What if we're all just aspects of some greater, unified self? You are the dominant aspect, I am higher self, Riker is our idealized self, Data is our intelligence and Troi is our heart, Worf is our barely contained fear and rage, and we are held together by this bubble of artificial context we call the Starship Enterprise, on a great trek across the vast expanse of a shoreless sea. Perhaps we are not a ship and crew at all, but a single entity on a voyage of personal discovery.

Picard
(sets down his glass and stands)
There's room for two in that torpedo tube, Guinan.

Picard exits.

What Is Enlightenment?

> Waking up is unpleasant, you know. You are nice and comfortable in bed. It is irritating to be woken up. That's the reason the wise guru will not attempt to wake people up. I hope I'm going to be wise here and make no attempt whatsoever to wake you up if you are asleep. It is really none of my business, even though I say to you at times, "Wake up!" My business is to do my thing, to dance my dance. If you profit from it fine; if you don't, too bad. As the Arabs say, "The nature of rain is the same, but it makes thorns grow in the marshes and flowers in the gardens."
>
> *Anthony de Mello*

INDULGE ME FOR A MOMENT as, in the interest of accuracy (but at the risk of appearing arrogant), I speak candidly. I am *(ahem)* spiritually enlightened. Sorry to be blunt, but it's a stone-cold fact. I am truth-realized. I am awake. My eyes are open. I see all that is and nothing that's not. I know all that's true and nothing that's false. I am a perfect master. My state is absolute; I can have equals but no superiors. Okay? Okay.

Was that too arrogant? Do you think my pathetic ego needs you to believe I'm special so I can believe it too? I hope you can see through all that, especially since these arrogant statements are not about me personally but about my impersonal condition, and would apply equally to any awakened being.

What I am *not* is a person as we think of a person as being. In fact, I barely qualify as a person at all. What's more, by prevailing standards I barely qualify as a spiritual teacher either, which is unmistakably ironic.

Rather than a person or a teacher, I am function. I am a tool that has been crafted for one particular job, a key that has been ground to fit one particular lock. I was born to become the tool, I became the tool, and now I am the tool. However whoever uses me for whatever is not my concern. I perform my function as it amuses me to do so because my function and my amusement follow the same arc. I do not work for myself or for you, but for the ocean of being in which we frolic.

Here's why I think people who like my books like my books. One, I'm a funny guy. No, wait... One, I'm the real deal. Two, I'm a funny guy. Three, I think people who like my books are relieved to find someone who makes sense where they'd come to believe no sense was possible. I think people want to stop wallowing in bullshit, at least for a little while. I think that some-where deep inside, there's a Little Bastard inside every seeker that knows they're trapped in an endless maze with no exits, and that all their running around is just running out the clock. I doubt that many readers even care about becoming enlightened, they probably just want to rise up above the maze for a minute. They just want a little understanding.

And a little understanding can go a long way. By simply understanding the limits of knowledge, we can destroy God. By understanding that nothing does not exist, we can destroy death. By understanding that two is not possible, we can destroy the universe. And by understanding that consciousness is all, we can destroy ourselves.

Of course, a statement like 'two is not possible' isn't a magical incantation. Having a conceptual grasp of nonduality, for instance, just means you have a tool. Now comes the hard work of actually using it to dis-mantle the parts of your dreamstate for which it's the *right* tool. I point this out because it seems like a lot of people think grasping a concept means the work is done, whereas it only means that the real work can begin. Epiphanies, realizations and insights aren't pre-cious gems, they're wrecking balls.

And what those statements – two is not possible, nothing does not exist, consciousness is all, etc – have in common is that they're all arrived at through simple reason. We don't need to abdicate our self-sovereignty to ancient teachings in foreign tongues requiring translators and intermediaries to bridge time and space and culture. Everything we need is readily available to direct apprehension. It's all about you, and you *are* you, so what do you need anyone else for?

The one who gunks everything up and makes it all seem so remote and inaccessible is Maya. Regardless of what you may believe, Maya is the teacher and the teaching. She is the Buddha, she is Mohammed and Jesus, she is the guru, she is the internet satsang instructor, she is the spiritual magazine publisher, she is the website that sends you daily tips about increasing mindfulness and decreasing stress. Whoever you're sure is *not* Maya is definitely Maya, probably including me in some subtle way. She has stacked the deck against you, so if you want to see past her, you have some serious reshuffling to do.

I don't mean you have to silence your thoughts more or take your meditation deeper; those are just sleep-inducing activities that were prescribed for you by masked Maya in the first place. You're already snuggled down in the dreamstate, and snuggling down further is not the way out. I mean that if you want to see, you have to open your eyes, which is just a way of saying you have to stop believing you think and start actually thinking.

Maya is the genius behind the illusion, and the journey of awakening is the process of tearing her veils away, one at a time. That's how awakening works; it's a process of continuously tearing away the next veil, and because those veils are actually the stuff of which you are made, it hurts.

☀

Ask a billion spiritual seekers what enlightenment is and what sort of word cloud would their answers form? The big words toward the middle might be bliss, unity, love, and happiness, surrounded by medium-sized words like knowing, wise, sagacious, and compassionate. The smallest, outermost words might be kind, gentle, serene, open, insightful, heart-centered, giving, and so forth.

But enlightenment is none of these things. It is not something more but everything less. Take away all of someone's delusions, all their beliefs and attachments, all their adherence to the illusion of segregated being, in short, wake them up from the dreamstate, and that person will be enlightened. All they will have left is their base programming to tell them what to do. I do this writing thing. Another might go off by themselves and play the cello. Another might be a librarian-gardener who never has a spiritual thought or utters a spiritual word. Another might tolerate the presence and endure the questions of spiritual seekers. But what no enlightened individual would be is engaged. They would not be capable of perceiving wrongness and would therefore have no possible interest in making anything right. They would have no skin in the game, no dog in the hunt, no emotional connection with which to animate 2D appearance into 3D reality. They would be an impartial and indifferent witness while retaining the base-level feelings and empathy inherent to the organism. They would not give a shit about compassion or serenity or bliss. They would see the absolute and unalterable rightness of everything and that nothing should be other than as it is. They would know the empty drama of life for what it is and feel no need to meddle in it. Whatever function they performed, they would know it to be the equivalent of digging one hole to fill another, but they would perform it anyway because, why not?

If someone who didn't speak your language tried to convince you they did, how successful would they be? Not very, right? They wouldn't complete a single sentence before you realized that they were trying to fool you. Even if they memorized a few phrases, how far would they get before you figured out they were faking? Ten seconds? Thirty? As soon as they opened their mouth, you'd see through the lie, not because you're a genius lie-detector or a hotshot linguist, but simply because, within the context of your language, you and this would-be deceiver inhabit different realms of comprehension.

What if a blind person tried to convince you they could see? How long before you noticed they couldn't?

It depends on whether you cared or not, I suppose. If you were watching them to see if they could see, you'd see through them pretty quickly. If you didn't care it might take longer.

It's like this for me in spiritual matters. I have perfect pitch. I can detect the slightest false note without trying. No one who isn't awake can convince me that they are. No one can convince me their eyes are open if they're not. No one can convince me that they dwell in my paradigm if they're still in the dreamstate. I can't be deceived in this regard any more than a blind man could make you believe he sees. This would be true of any awakened being.

Of course, we are seldom confronted with people who claim to speak a language they don't, or pretend to be sighted if they're not. No one goes around misrepresenting themselves so blatantly. The only way to get away with such a transparent lie is if there's no one who knows the truth who can call you out, so there's really no area in which you could possibly deceive all the people all the time.

Except one. In modern spirituality, you can declare yourself an expert because there's no one to stand up and expose you. You pick up the patter, develop a few signature talking points and a few catchphrases, leech off of someone else's credibility for the price of a framed photo, maybe adopt a stage name and tweak your appearance, and congratulations, you're a spiritual teacher. It's like a poker game in which all the players are bluffing and no one is calling, or like competing magicians who have a shared interest in keeping trade secrets. You can argue that magicians are knowing deceivers and spiritual teachers are just unwitting links in a chain of deception, but who cares about them? Your only concern is you.

Whenever I peek into the world of spirituality, I am surprised and maybe a bit disheartened by how many false teachers are out there and the high regard in which they're held. Popular teachings fall into a narrow range between ridiculous nonsense and intriguing nonsense, often revolving around thoughts, feelings, realizations, levels of consciousness, and a lot of esoteric concepts and flowery talk. Where there's a dialog between teacher and student, it often looks like emotional counseling with a spiritual twist. Where there's a teaching, it's as if students were supposed to learn and understand rather than do. What these teachers *don't* seem to teach is what the process of awakening really is and what it really entails because, one, they have no idea, and two, their students would bolt for the exits if they caught sight of the real thing, and without students you can't play teacher. When you're not the real deal, you can't use the stick; you have to be liked.

I'm not opposed to false teachers. I have no issue with them. They perform their function and I perform mine, and there's surprisingly little overlap between the two. I'm not surprised that their world of spirituality is basically one gigantic disinformation machine; that makes perfect sense to me. What surprises me, frankly, is that I get to do what I do. That makes less sense to me. Truth has no place in the dreamstate.

The word enlightenment has devolved over time to mean something quite unrelated to awakening from the dreamstate, something involving contentment and happiness, muted thoughts and pleasant feelings, minor revelations and petty insights, and pretty much whatever the audience would like it to mean. That's why we have so many spiritual teachers running around, because we've redefined the term enlightenment to be much more open and inclusive. We've democratized the journey of awakening, turned it into a nice, safe theme park in which all the rides drop you off right where you got on.

But the real enlightenment is perfectly cut and dried. There are no partial awakenings, no stages or levels. One is either awake or asleep. One's eyes are open or closed. One is in the dreamstate paradigm or out of it. In a similar vein, there are no variations or types of awakening. There is not this kind and that kind, there is only awake from the dreamstate or not. The awakened state is not the exclusive domain of any sect or religion or culture, or even of the human race. It is the domain of all self-aware beings.

I estimated at one point that out of a hundred million people, maybe one might be awake. Let's say that translates to 60-80 enlightened people on the Earth at the moment. Is that still what I think? No, I'd guess much lower now. I can name a dozen living people who are awake, seven of them unknown. I can name maybe three dozen ever. I'm not a collector though, and the authentic cases would be the least conspicuous, so my guess is certainly low. My actual guess would be two dozen at present, and even that feels high. If some trustworthy spiritual census showed more, I'd be surprised. If it showed more than fifty, I'd fall out of my chair.

So then, who are all these hundreds and thousands of disseminators of faux-spirituality teaching in ashrams and satsangs, publishing books and videos and blogs, sitting on mountaintops dispensing remedies for restlessness?

They are Maya. She is legion.

There is no other enlightenment than awake from the dreamstate, and those who say there is are lying or deceived. Either way, they are not your friends. (Or maybe they *are* your friends and *I'm* not because they're trying to protect you from the flames I'm encouraging you to step into.) Enlightenment is black and white and plain as day. It's as unmistakable as the difference between sighted and blind, awake and asleep. As convincing and sincere and revered as they may be, the fact is that nearly all teachers of enlightenment are unenlightened, self-deluded and dreamstate-bound. Given a list of the top few hundred experts in the field of spirituality, with the most idolized and venerated at the top, even *I* would be surprised at who got crossed off and how few remained.

I am not in competition with anyone. I don't say these things to diminish others or elevate myself, I am simply pointing out what you're up against in trying to hack your way out of the tangled forest of delusion. What I'm describing is what you'll see for yourself if you look for yourself. Trust no one. You have no friends. You have no ally but yourself and you are your own worst enemy. And you're asleep. And you don't know it because you're dreaming that you're awake.

There are no good guys or bad guys, just different functions. Spiritual teachers form a human shield to protect spiritual seekers from venturing too far from the herd and too close to the edge, which is a valid dreamstate function, but there are also just enough authentic teachers around to let you know that if you want to blow this joint, you can.

The Champions of Delusion

> Unless it comes out of your soul like a rocket,
> unless being still would drive you to madness or
> suicide or murder, don't do it. Unless the sun
> inside you is burning your gut, don't do it.
> When it is truly time, and if you have been
> chosen, it will do it by itself and it will keep on
> doing it until you die or it dies in you. There is
> no other way. And there never was.

Charles Bukowski

I AM ADDRESSING SOMEONE ELSE'S GROUP that I haven't addressed before, so I don't know them and, except for the books, they don't know me. The theme of the gathering is nonduality rather than, say, angelic ascension or yogic twirling, so I'm not too out of place.

There's a chair for me but I don't care to sit when I speak. I pace back and forth before the group casually answering questions and asking some of my own for a few minutes.

I enjoy a certain amount of freedom when speaking to groups of people I won't have to see again. I can experiment with saying things differently, a little more forcefully or experimentally, just to see how it's received and what it leads to. If I go too far and burn the group or trash myself in their eyes, it doesn't matter. It's not my chance to teach something, it's my chance to learn something about the tricky business of conveying truth.

After half an hour of small talk, one guy stands up and launches into a whole thing about his heart, his feeling of openness maybe, something about a song from his childhood, his surprise at how his experience of spiritual awakening was different from what he'd expected, his state of joy, I think, or maybe his understanding that everything was joy, something like that. Based on his experience, he seemed to think he was now awake, which he was not. He went back to the thing about the song, like some primal song of life that kept welling up in him. I interrupted before he could start singing.

"Okay, fine, that's great," I say, a bit unclear as to what he was trying to say, "but it's all just something you experienced, right? Or that you're experiencing now?"

"For the last few weeks," he says.

"Okay," I say, "but it's just an experience, is what I'm asking. That's okay, go ahead and sit down. I once knew a guy who said he drank water from a crystal cup and became enlightened for three months. He wanted my help getting back to that state, which he described as such profound bliss that he couldn't care for himself. I told him he didn't need me, he needed that crystal cup. I didn't bother telling him that enlightenment wasn't a state of consciousness and that all he'd had was an experience. Who cares about an experience? All experience is in the dreamstate so who cares? Waking up isn't about your experience or your happiness or anything like that. That's all just makyo, shit, a mental-emotional waste product. You don't sift through it or make mud pies or bring it to show-and-tell, you flush it down the toilet and keep going. This is for all of you now. Awakening from the dreamstate has nothing to do with your experience or your feelings, and there is no other enlightenment than waking up from the dreamstate. You are not in the process of becoming anything or achieving anything. You are not on a path to super-awesomeness. All you can do is rid yourself of bullshit, and you don't do that by silencing your thoughts or having peak experiences or drinking from crystal cups. If you want to be happy, go do drugs or fall in love or win the lottery. If you want to wake up, you have to stop being asleep."

This stirs some people up a bit, which is good. Several stand up and start talking about things that I don't recognize as being worth talking about. I'm not a counselor or a girlfriend or a bartender, so most stuff about feelings and experiences make my eyes glaze over.

"You have some issues?" I finally respond to the trend before it can sap my energy. "So what? We all have issues. This isn't about issues. Issues are emotional demons and the only thing an emotional demon wants to do is hold you back, that's how they win. You think you have to defeat your demons, but all they want is for you to engage them so they can keep you at their level; then they have won and you have lost. That's what I see going on here right now. This stuff is not what it appears; this is ego at work keeping you thrashing around in the sewer instead of climbing out of it. Your issues don't mean shit, your past doesn't mean shit, your adventures in consciousness don't mean shit. This is about going forward or not, making progress or not, destroying layers of delusion or staying trapped inside them. As long as you think you have to deal with every bit of emotional detritus, you're effectively stuck right where you are. You feel the impulse to magnify things, to zoom in and study them in microscopic detail, and I'm telling you to zoom out, pull back out of yourself and your body, out of your family and friendships, out of your house and town and country, keep zooming back off the planet, out of the solar system and the galaxy, all the way out past time and space to total nothingness. That's what nonduality refers to; awareness without appearance, consciousness without content. That's your true home. That's probably not what you want to hear, I get that, but that's the deal. There are powerful emotional forces working to keep you zoomed in on petty details, but you have to think your way past those forces and zoom out if you ever want to do what you say you want to do by coming here."

There's more arguing and resistance from the group and several suggestions that I take my negative brand of spirituality and fuck the fuck off. I drink water and sit for a minute and let them squabble. Some think I know what I'm talking about and some think I'm full of the same shit I'm saying they're full of. When things settle down a bit, a middle-aged guy, very soft and gentle-looking, stands up and describes an issue he's having with his thoughts or his mind or something.

"I'm trying not to think so much," he explains. "It seems like I'm always thinking, even though I try not to. I want to quiet my thoughts and be more mindful, but it seems like my mind keeps wanting to be active all the time."

"Well," I say, standing again, pacing again, "I can't address the mindfulness thing, but I can address the active mind issue by saying that sounds great. That's a great problem to have. Your brain is eager to do some thinking so why not go ahead and do some thinking?

Your brain is not your enemy. Your brain is not trying to derail your spiritual quest, it's your fearful heart that does that by telling you to sit down and close your eyes and silence your mind. Your emotions hold you in stasis between desire and fear, but your brain just wants to think, to attack problems and make things make sense. Your brain is like a dog that wants to chew on a bone and you keep telling this wonderful dog to sit, to stay, to shut up. But why shut the dog up? It's the dog's nature to chew bones, to rip stuff apart. Why deny its nature? Let's toss the dog a bone and see what happens. I can think of a few bones right off hand, like what's this mindfulness bullshit? You'll be mindful when you're awake, but you won't wake up by being mindful. Let the dog chew on that for awhile and see what's left."

The nice middle-aged guy starts to reply but there's nothing for him to say except that he disagrees with me. The only reason he disagrees with me is because he bought into some bad ideas and wants to defend his bad decisions.

"Don't respond, it's okay, sit down please. I know what you're thinking. You're thinking that being spiritual means you have to be peaceful and serene and contemplative, that your inner being is supposed to be calm and tranquil, that you have to silence your thoughts, that kind of thing. But that's nothing, that's just something from a late night spiritual infomercial. Forget all that nonsense. Sorry, but I'm not the one who sold it to you, I'm just telling you that you've been scammed. There's no fixing it, you just have to climb out of the hole you dug yourself into and get on the right track. This is war and you must become a warrior. Me, I *like* thinking, I *like* the brain and I want to use it to set the world on fire, to burn the whole thing down, kill God, kill Buddha, kill your ego-self. You're not getting out of this alive so why not play a good game? Why not let the dog off the leash? Let it run. Your brain wants to think and some guru tells you to silence your thoughts. Seriously, ask yourself, which one sounds right to you? If one guy tells you to think as hard as you can, in the best way you can, and another guy tells you to silence your thoughts because thinking is bad and a silent mind is good, which one of those guys sounds like he's selling some bullshit? Even if he believes it himself, okay? Close your eyes, silence your mind, repeat a mantra, heart good, brain bad, what does that sound like? That guy who's telling you not to use your head sounds like a flimflam man selling you a timeshare in paradise, the kind of pitch you'd only fall for in the middle of the night. And now look at the absolute failure of human spirituality to help anyone realize truth and see if you can draw a connection between those two things; between these purveyors of delusion that send everyone in exactly the wrong direction and the perfect failure of seekers to find the only thing that can never be lost. Is it any wonder that you're asking me how to turn your brain off? Is it any wonder that even Zen and Advaita don't help anyone wake up? Of course not. It's exactly what you'd expect from Maya's champions of delusion. The unstated goal of all spirituality and religion is to keep everyone happily asleep in the dreamstate. This is not orchestrated on the human level, this is ego at work, Maya, and what is Maya but the same perfect intelligence we see at work in all things at all times? The entire dreamstate runs on perfect intelligence and the ego-self is as much a part of that intelligence as oceans and galaxies. That's what you're dealing with, that's what you're up against. That's what we see happening when you come here to me and ask how to turn your brain off. I mean, how insane is that? It's totally batshit crazy from the perspective of awakening from delusion, but it's absolutely ingenious from the perspective of protecting people capable of thought from going where thought inevitably leads, which is straight out of delusion, straight out of the dreamstate. You want to silence your mind? Put a bullet in it. Why not? You're not using it anyway so what's the difference? Then you'll be serene as a corpse. Then your mind will be perfectly silent and you will be more enlightened than any master who ever lived and exactly as enlightened as your dead goldfish when you flushed it down the toilet. Maya has to demonize the mind, vilify thought, outlaw common sense. Common sense is all it takes to awaken from the dreamstate because the dreamstate is intrinsically nonsensical. A simple thought can blow the whole thing to pieces which is why everything is arrayed against thinking. You don't have to silence your mind and achieve higher consciousness to wake up, you just have to apply some common sense, *use* your brain instead of suppressing it. And let me remind you all right now that I'm not saying that my version of enlightenment is better than anyone else's, I'm saying there's only one version and anyone promoting anything else is working for the opposition. Awakening from the dreamstate, from the illusion of self, is the only enlightenment there is. It is clear and specific and unmistakable. There are no varieties or degrees of enlightenment, and there is no possibility of enlightenment inside the dreamstate, I hope you see that. You can't be spiritually enlightened and not be truth-realized, I hope that makes sense to you. I know they sold you on this idea of transcendent happiness, but enlightenment is not a peak state. It's a paradigm shift from false to true, from asleep to awake. You're either awake from the dreamstate or you're still a prisoner of delusion, and there is no such thing as an enlightened person because to be enlightened is to have detached from the illusion of personhood, the ego-self."

I pause to catch my breath and drink some water. No one starts squabbling this time.

"Is everyone fairly clear on all this?" I continue. "Thank you for nodding. Okay, that was fun. Good topic. I don't want to address this point anymore, anyone got anything else? Don't be shy, say what's on your mind. Try to offend me if that makes it easier, try to contradict me or prove me wrong about something. Believe me, I'll love you if you can do it. You can't, but I'd be thrilled out of my mind if you could. I can tell you stuff about your reality all day because my eyes are open and yours aren't, but if you could tell me something about mine, something I don't see or haven't looked at or didn't know, that would be like discovering a new world for me. Again, you can't do it, but it's a cool challenge, right? Lighten up, let's just accept the fact the today is not about being mellow and soothing and let's take this opportunity to slap ourselves around a little and see what happens. Dueling dharma, right? Satsang fight club, why not? The first rule of satsang fight club is, today is a good day to die. Go ahead and get agitated. You'll survive."

Someone in the back of the room is crying. I can't tell if it's in response to something I said or if they're just going through something or maybe giving birth. "Boil some water!" I am about to command. "Bring clean sheets!" But then I see it's a guy and figure he's probably not having a baby.

A very spiritual looking woman of around forty and wrapped in a colorful shawl stands up.

"I agree with the woman who wrote the letter in the front of your second book," she says. "I don't think you have a spiritual bone in your body."

I nod vigorously in agreement.

"I know, right? Maybe I don't, but I'm telling you the obvious truth compared to all your gurus and spiritually-boned teachers who are telling you convoluted lies. What does it mean if what I say is true? Just hypothetically, what does it mean if the totally unspiritual guy is right and all the lovely teachers and graybeard gurus are full of shit? Seekers far more dedicated than you have been achieving failure for millennia, are you sure you want to keep following the same path they took? The battle here is between mind and heart, and heart has always won because heart has energy and mind doesn't, unless it can somehow rally the heart to its cause which, I assure you, is the only way it'll ever work. Hatred versus fear, that's how it can work, now we have a fair fight. Fear still has the advantage because hatred derives its power from fear, but now we're all on the same playing field, the field of Kurukshetra, right? That's where this game is played, that's where this battle is fought. Completely inside. Totally inward. There's no one here but you, never was. Two massive armies facing each other. Everyone on both sides is an aspect of you, and they all have to die. Other than this battle there is nothing. Every other spiritual activity is bullshit. No amount of meditation or knowledge or consciousness exploration or anything else matters in the least, only this battle between these two warring factions inside you. And what does this internal battle look like? It looks like suicide, of course, because that's what it is. One side of you is trying to die and the other is trying to survive. This is a protracted battle with many casualties and a lot of pain. There's really no point in explaining all this, but I explain a lot of things there's no point in explaining. You'll find out for yourself or you won't, that's all. You do that, any of you, and then you tell me what you think about all those teachers and gurus with all their closed eyes and quiet minds. You'll want to strangle them. You won't believe you believed them. Sure, we all love peace and serenity, and if that's what you want then the spiritual marketplace is eager to serve, but if you're thinking of becoming a truth-seeker, a serious person, then I'm telling you what that looks like. It looks like killing yourself very slowly and very painfully, and having nothing to show for it when you're done. Okay? Thanks for the comment. Anyone else got anything? Something? Nothing? You know, coming together in a group like this is just an evasive maneuver; ego cloaking itself in spirituality as a way of preempting any possibility of awakening. From what I can tell, spiritual teachers like to explain things, as if they were teaching you to be awake, as if the only thing that stood between you and awaken-ing was more knowledge or a better understanding, but it's your so-called knowledge and understanding – beliefs, opinions, wrong-knowing – that forms the barrier between the dreamstate and the awakened state. That's why you gather in groups, too. Anytime you come together like this you're taking refuge against the threat of awakening. That's why you come here, not to initiate the dissolution of the ego-self, but to further reinforce it by deepening your entrenchment. If you wanted to wake up you'd be off by yourself doing it, not clumping together like frightened sheep trembling at the sound of a distant wolf. All of religion and spirituality is really just a ring of protective custody holding you safely away from the outer rim of the dreamstate. You don't come here to wake up, as you like to pretend, you come here to stay asleep, so that's pretty interesting, right? You're just here indulging vanity, seeking happiness, finding inner peace and all that. I mean, I don't expect you all to go home and begin the real process of awakening just because some loudmouth jerk told you your spiritual life is an elaborate fraud, but who knows? Maybe one of you is listening. Maybe one of you is lying in bed tonight thinking, 'Geez, am I really full of shit? Am I doing all this spiritual stuff out of fear? Am I lying to myself about everything? Am I really just afraid of change? Am I desperate to hold onto something that's not really mine in the first place? What's the point of my life if the whole thing is a lie?' That's what it sounds like when the Little Bastard starts waking up inside you, and if he gets riled up, then life as you know it will be over. The horn will be blown and the battle will commence. If that happens, you will experience a few years of raging internal conflict followed by a decade of processing the aftermath, and then you will know the inner peace that can only be found in perfect desolation. And the funny thing is, at a subconscious level you already know all this, which is to say, your *ego-self* knows it, and that's why you're really here, to make sure that nothing as horrible as awakening from the dreamstate can ever happen to you. Or, you know, maybe not. Anyway, food for thought. Anyone else have anything you want to talk about? I think this is going pretty well. Any more questions? Hello? Don't everybody jump up at once."

Starship Gita

Act 3: The Holodeck

Picard and Ned McFeely on the Holodeck. Ned is dressed in sandals, cargo shorts, and a t-shirt that says "God was my co-pilot but we crashed in the mountains and I ate him." He stands on a path beside a trickling mountain stream amid lush green surroundings. Picard, in uniform, approaches.

PICARD

Are you Ned McFeely?

NED

Sure, why not.

PICARD

My name is Jean-Luc Picard. I can't say more
for the moment...

NED

I know who you are, Captain. And this is a
Holodeck?

PICARD

Uh, it is, yes. How did you know that?

NED

The dreamstate by any other name...
(examines his hands)
So I'm not really here? My sense of self-awareness is an illusion?

PICARD

I'm afraid so. Technically, you don't even have
a sense of self-awareness, it's just something you
say. You are a product of the computer, com-
piled from historical records. You have no independent reality.

NED

What a drag. And what about *your* sense of self-
awareness, Captain?

PICARD

Oh, mine is quite real, I assure you. You are
merely a holographic projection, whereas I
actually exist in the real world.

NED

Sure, let's go with that. Computer, end program.

No change.

PICARD

You can't give that order.

NED

You might be surprised.

PICARD

Apparently not. Listen, Mr. McFeely, we are
presently confronted with a situation...

NED

Yeah, the Borg. Congratulations.

Ned begins to stroll along the mountain path. Picard
accompanies him.

PICARD

How do you know about the Borg?

NED

Why else would you have the computer generate a historical figure who defeated them?

PICARD

So you *did* defeat the Borg!

NED

Not like you think. I'm afraid the Borg are
not just the enemy of the moment, Captain,

they are your perfect antagonist, your negative image, the yin to your yang or yang to your yin, something like that. They represent the other side of the false equation which defines your existence. In order to defeat them, you must defeat yourself. It's not a war but a rectification. This conflict is a sign of imbalance, and one way or another, balance will be restored.

PICARD

We must resist them!

NED

(stops walking, faces Picard)

To the degree that you resist, they are empowered. Whatever you withhold, they will find. Whatever you extend, they will cut off. Whatever you cherish, they will consume. Yes, Captain, you can defeat the Borg, but the price of that victory is everything.

PICARD

Everything?

NED

(shrugs)

Everything, nothing; same thing. It's just a matter of perspective. Gateless gate stuff.

They continue walking.

PICARD

But here you are. You fought them! You won!

NED

I merely rectified the equation. And, as you have pointed out, I do not exist. That is my victory. If it's any comfort, this too shall pass. Balance is always restored in the end.

PICARD

I have no time for riddles, Mr. McFeely! Our records indicate that you were one of the last proponents of an authentic Nonduality, which seems to be some archaic system of self-discovery.

NED

Alas, the thing one discovers is that there's no self to discover. Yes, I was there for the brief heyday of Nonduality, but then the internet came along and unleashed an army of Tribbles – something akin to your Borg, but warm and fuzzy – creating a viral degradation that reduced Nonduality from a force of awakening to an agent of sleep. These Tribbles were unwitting purveyors of disinformation that turned the battle cry of freedom into a whimper for peace. Through a process of emotional alchemy, Nonduality was converted from a corrosive acid into a sugary soft-drink, making it the perfect carrier for the disease it was meant to cure.

PICARD

I don't care about any of that.

NED

Because you don't understand the conflict in which you're engaged. You don't know where this battle is really fought. The Borg are irrelevant. The true enemy is always within, between your heart and your mind; between what you believe, wish and fear, and what you know; between dreaming with eyes closed and seeing with eyes open.

PICARD

Then how do I know if I'm fighting a real battle with the Borg, or if I'm fighting this internal conflict you describe?

NED

There's really no difference. Guinan told you your options; assimilate or die. Geordi told you the third; transcend.

PICARD

How do you know what they said?

NED

Because you are all characters in a drama of which I am the author. Your computer brought us together here because that's how I wrote the scene. You are in uniform because I said so. I could have put you in a pinafore. You are my puppet.

PICARD

I can assure you, Mr. McFeely, that you are not the author of me! You are merely a creation of the ship's computer.

Ned

That's an amusing thought. I am the creation of a computer of which I am the author; the Vyasa-Krishna paradox. Okay, check it out, so these two snakes are eating each other...

Picard

Enough! You say you are the author, then prove it! Change this situation. Eradicate the Borg from existence!

Ned

But as you say, Captain, there is no me. I am not here. And even if I did exist, nothing could be done to alter your situation. Accounts must be balanced, there must be a reckoning. You stand at the brink, not of some trifling battle, but of your own escape from captivity. This is it, the process is in motion. Nothing can stop it now.

Picard

Christ, I may as well be talking to Data's cat.

Ned

Okay, Captain, so I'm a computer-generated character, correct? Despite the infinite appearance, this finite Holodeck is the full extent of my reality?

Picard

Yes, that is correct.

NED

I only exist within an artificial context outside of which I cannot exist?

PICARD

Of course! Now stop wasting time and focus on the matter at hand!

NED

Then ask yourself, what is *your* context? What is the framework outside of which *you* cannot exist?

PICARD

You mean, this ship? The Enterprise?

NED

At the moment. Just as I dwell within the artificial context of the Holodeck and cannot exist outside of it, so are you always within an artificial context outside of which you cannot exist. You are always contained within a false context, always protectively walled off from the truth of the infinite.

PICARD

Meaning what, exactly?

NED

Meaning, you came to me for advice and my advice is always this; check your assumptions. Now, can Data's cat do this? *Computer, delete program Ned McFeely.*

Ned and the mountain scene disappear. Picard stands

alone in the blank gridwork of the Holodeck.

PICARD

Not so fast, dammit! Computer, resume program Ned McFeely!

COMPUTER

Program Ned McFeely does not exist.

Yolanda Periwinkle

"I just want to be easy about this and
have a nice time. If we get to the part
where it's not easy, okay, but for now
we can be easy."

Marichelle

I WANT TO SAY THINGS RIGHT but I'm not interested in convincing you of anything. Convincing
is not a thing for me, I am just doing some talking for my own reasons. My wish is trying to say
things as well as I can. I am not trying to convince
you of anything, I'm just talking to get stuff out. I
have my own reasons for talking and saying things
good this one time.

I don't need for anyone to respect me or agree with me. I agree with myself is all. All I have to worry about is being right, which is no problem for me because I am not coma-based. My basis is correct so everything is correct. Everyone else, like all the experts you can think of, are all built on a faulty basis, so no matter how smart they are, their input is faulty so there is never valid output. I don't have bad input, so that's my advantage.

My calculations are not based on believing coma is reality. No one who thinks coma is reality can ever be right about anything. If you could understand just that one thing it would change everything, but maybe you don't want everything to change which is okay too.

You can't agree with this but I don't let that stop me from saying it. As long as I am correct, nothing else matters. I have no other thing to worry about. Believe me, if the whole world laughs at me, this gets a yawn from me. Same if the whole world raises me to the highest pedestal. What do I care? I don't change my lunch plans for either thing. I am not subject to opinion. You don't understand this, but if you did, I wouldn't even have to say it. That's how obvious it is.

To understand anything is very easy. The trick is not to believe things you don't know, okay? Once you do that then no more mystery. You make a lot of mystery just by believing things you don't know. There is no real mystery anywhere. Hard to believe, I know.

There are no facts in coma, so if you think there are some facts you need to look for you should go think some more. When you turn on the lights you are not right away looking at all sorts of facts about everything, you are just seeing what's real for the first time instead of things you believe. You might not like what you see. It's nice to sit in the dark with a lot of friends.

You can't say I'm wrong because I don't really say anything. You say everything, I don't say anything. So if you want to say I'm wrong all you're saying is that you want to stay in your coma, which I already know. It's like life and death to you to stay in your coma. I understand this.

You and me sitting here would seem very similar to someone else, like we are similar people, but to me we are not the same. You are stuck in a tiny little coma and I am out here in the open. You are wrong about everything and I can't be wrong about anything. I know that sounds wrong to you, but I can't be worried about how it sounds to you right now. I am trying to say things right. I can worry about you or I can say things right. I can't do both.

Okay, so for one thing, this is not a conversation we are having right now. You may think so, but you and me right now are not in the same reality because you are in coma and I am not. I remember enough from my coma time to know that some things I say may cause upset, but there is no cause for upset, there is only cause for waking up if you want to, or staying in coma if you want to. It doesn't matter what you do.

You think I think you're real because I am talking to you, but really no. I have no opinion about you. Just because I am here in coma doing coma things doesn't make me be in coma like you now or like

I was. I can still be here but it's not the same. I'm not really here. Neither are you, by the way.

You think everything is just the way you see it, but there is a much simpler explanation. If you want to know everything you just open your eyes and look. But you don't know your eyes are closed and you're in coma, so that's a problem. Maybe I count to three and snap my fingers and you wake up, but you can't do it that way. There's only one way and it's not much fun. If you have something else to do I would do that.

You don't know you're in coma right now, you think you live in reality. The thing about coma is you think it's real. As long as you think it's real then you are a slave of this coma you live in. I am not in coma. I know where I am and you're not here.

I would say the conversation about why we can't have a conversation is more interesting than the conversation you want to have. You want me to say things that make sense to you, but you don't need me for that. I'm no good for that. Maybe my job here is to say things that don't make sense to you. But for you to like what I say is not a thing. This is not for your opinion or belief. Really the opposite, I would say.

I want to be very soft and friendly in the way I talk with you. I know other ways and I don't like them, even if they're better really. I just want to be easy about this and have a nice time. If we get to the part where it's not easy, okay, but for now we can be easy.

I can't even talk to someone who thinks they're a human being. It's like talking to a stump. Why talk to a stump? When you turn on the lights, all the human beings disappear. People who think they are human beings are not really alive, I would say. I see them in the market or the café or on the street and I think of them as scenery, like just for background or something. Obviously you can't talk to someone like that. It's like, stop being Yolanda Periwinkle for a minute so I can talk to you, okay? I don't know where I got that name but you know what I mean.

You ask how to be free of ego, but this is not the right question. This is a question you don't need from a tradition you don't need. There is no tradition that helps people get out of coma, I'm pretty sure. Any tradition must always be about the opposite. Maybe you really want the opposite, but if you want to come out from coma you will have no help or friends. All by yourself is the only way.

You go to traditions because you want to come back to safety. That is a good thing to want and they can help you with that, but when it's time to go you go alone. There is no one to help with that. No one can help with that. I can tell you some things, but you have to go alone.

You can have beginning, middle and end, or you can have end, beginning and middle, or middle, end and beginning. The middle is a good time for the beginning or the end, and the beginning can be the end, and the order can change. For the beginning to be the end is not so much fun, but things aren't always fun. There are not so many rules as you think, at least not the exact rules you think.

To ask how you can be free of ego is like asking how you can be free of your body. Why would you want to be free of your body? Has someone told you that it's bad to have a body? To me it seems wonderful to have a body. Look at all the wonderful things you can do with a body that you can't do without one. Maybe someday you don't have a body, then that's fine, then you can do other things, but now you have a body so you can do body things. If you don't have a body, how do you know what the temperature is? Can you drink soup without a body? I bet you can't. Can you even smell soup? I don't know how because you don't have a nose. You can't even tell if the soup is hot so you should blow on it first, right? No lips. Don't be so fast to give up your lips. Same with ego.

The Spiritual Anarchist

> He felt that his whole life was some kind of
> dream and he sometimes wondered whose it
> was and whether they were enjoying it.

Douglas Adams

I AM SITTING WITH KARL and his twin kids John
and Clare. We are having a little reunion lunch
celebrating their roles in *Theory*. The twins are both
learning to drive now, so that makes them however
old that makes them. John and Clare were eager to
participate during the time I lived over their garage
and wrote the book, and they seem even more eager
now that I have immortalized them in print, as if they
have inherited an obligation to your spiritual welfare.

They're finishing their pizza, winding things down, when they wind things back up.

"Do I have a Little Bastard?" asks Clare out of nowhere.

"Yeah, how about me?" adds John.

"I have one, right?" says Clare.

"How can I not?" asks John.

"I think I hear mine sometimes," says Clare.

"Mine tells me I'm not awake," says John.

"If I listen to him, will I be enlightened?" asks Clare.

"Is this how it starts?" asks John.

Karl looks at me sideways, like this is my fault.

The Little Bastard is the person inside the person, the authentic seeker behind the false facade which students outwardly project. The Little Bastard is the agitator, the spiritual anarchist, the crazy little bullshit-hater who wants to burn everything down to see what's left, and then burn that down too. It was always my impression when speaking with supposedly spiritual people that the outer person was just the camouflaged shell of that person's egoic defense system. All spiritual aspirants are engaged in this self-deception and that's why they fail at their stated goal of waking up while succeeding at their unstated goal of staying asleep.

The internal motivations of the spiritual seeker are very different from those on display. The outer person is just the cosmetic layer draped over the structural framework of ego. Enslaved by their own egoic imperatives, they are engaged *not* in the pursuit of waking up but in conspiring *against* it. Weird, I know, and weirder for you because you're probably engaged in this self-deception right now. I mean, right?

This is such a common phenomenon that it effectively defines the modern spiritual seeker. Sincerity and level of commitment mean nothing. Practice and technique mean nothing. Knowledge and understanding mean nothing. The only thing that means anything is if the suicidal maniac inside you is able to lure you to the edge of the abyss and give you a push when you're peering over.

Such is the inherently fraudulent nature of the teacher-student dynamic. In the *authentic* teacher-student dynamic, there is actually very little dynamic at all because the person making the journey doesn't need any help. Just like falling off a cliff; once you've taken that tricky first step, the rest is pretty self-explanatory. The false dynamic may require interaction with a teacher, but the authentic one is a solo thing.

The majority of people who have approached me to ask questions or request assistance have been playing the truthseeker *role* rather than actually seeking truth. This has always been fine with me because I still got what I wanted. I was never striving for success as a spiritual facilitator. I work for the books and all those interactions serve the books regardless of what, if any, fruit they bore.

Your ego will do anything to survive. It can make you believe anything, but it will not seek its own demise. If you understand that, then you understand that the spiritual marketplace is marvelously successful at performing the ego-preserving function of always promising and never delivering, and you'll understand why billions have sought and so few have found. More importantly, you will gain a valuable insight into your own situation.

Once I came to understand that students weren't really seekers and that spirituality was just a fear-based vanity ploy, I also came to understand that somewhere inside each student was the weak ray of hope that I came to think of as the Little Bastard. The Little Bastard is the authentic seeker, the tiny aspect of us that hates the endless forest of delusion and wants to burn it down, even though he must burn with it. Once I realized he was in there, I began directing my words less to the outer person and more to the scrappy Little Bastard within. The seeker is never authentic because that person is always ego-based and ego will never willingly undergo harm. The Little Bastard is the only hope, though whose hope he is remains an amusing question.

The Little Bastard is your spark of pure integrity. He has clarity but no power. The only power in the dreamstate is emotion, and until the Little Bastard can tap into that, he can never be more than a minor irritant with a voice so small that it can't be heard over the din of ego's constant self-projection. He is David whose tiny stone of truth can topple a seemingly invincible giant. He is your inner hero; a lonely little rebel standing up to Darth Vader, the Death Star, and a million clone army, and giving them all the finger.

Cool dude.

If he can somehow tap into the power of emotion, there is a possibility that the Little Bastard can grow large and formidable and become an influential being in his own right. The emotions he requires are not the pretty ones like love and happiness, but the savage ones like hatred and rage. Only the hatred of being a lie can ever overcome the fear of not being at all.

So, do John and Clare have a Little Bastard within? Even for them to wonder if he's in there suggests that he is. In what configuration of person is there no shred of doubt? Who is so certain that the dreamstate is true that they do not harbor a small voice which whispers in their ear "It's all bullshit. It's all bullshit."? But are John and Clare's Little Bastards in there, jumping up and down waving his arms and trying to get my attention? Not really. I know what that looks like and this isn't it. But that doesn't mean he's not in there, sitting in the dark, lonely and confused.

"Sure," I tell them, "that's probably what's motivating you guys; some tiny inner demon is creating an agitation inside you, like a splinter in your mind, right? Well, that's what the Little Bastard is, he's that splinter in your mind telling you something's not right. Everything else might be telling you everything is just fine, but this one tiny voice in your head keeps telling you it's not."

Karl looks at me pointedly. I know what he's saying. "Don't drag my kids too far into all this. Their mother will kill me if I don't bring them home normal." I get it, but this is all pretty safe. John and Clare are very polite and their interest is playful. If I ran a One-Hour Martinizing service, they'd be just as interested in non-flammable solvents. I'm just the amusing distraction of the moment.

On the other hand, if John and Clare *do* have a Little Bastard and he *is* trying to get my attention, then I would be remiss to dismiss their interest as juvenile or polite. Just because they're young doesn't mean they're out of play, and I have no obligation to their parents in this regard. The Little Bastard may be there, inside them, asking me to give him something to work with, something he can use to turn a spark into a flame. If the Little Bastard asks, I have some weird obligation to answer. If the answer gets ignored or goes unheeded, that's not my problem, but not answering would be not-right. I am a firestarter and a friend of arsonists. If someone asks me for a light, I give it to them. The question is, can I provide covert support to the nascent rebel alliance within these children? Can I give John and Clare something that they can use to start a fire if they want to or ignore if they don't?

Yeah, I can do that.

☼

"What does the Little Bastard look like?" asks John.

"How can we tell if we have one?" asks Clare.

"Can you give a for instance?" asks John.

"An example," says Clare.

I think about it for a moment. I like to use our shared stories whenever possible, and that means movies. You've seen *The Matrix,* for instance, and it's an easier way to explain Plato's cave allegory than asking you to read Plato. Two movies come to mind to help describe the Little Bastard, but one of them, *How to Get Ahead In Advertising*, is a bit obscure so I go with the other one.

"There's a pretty popular movie where we see what happens when the Little Bastard gains a foothold, when he gets born into the world and becomes a fullblown character instead of just a squeaky demon. It's like giving birth to your own inner spiritual master. That's what I did, and it's probably the only way anyone can ever manage to awaken; not with any external guru, but by unleashing their own inner guru."

"What movie?" asks John.

"What character?" asks Clare.

"Tyler Durden," I say.

"Coooool!" says John.

"Fight Club!" says Clare.

Your Little Bastard is awake inside you, trying to get your attention, hoping to someday firebomb your bullshit life the same way Tyler Durden firebombed Edward Norton's bullshit apartment. It's your Little Bastard that knows you're full of shit and that you don't have to be. It's him who's trying to wake you up and it's him that ego keeps suppressed at all costs because ego is a strawman and is deathly afraid of fire. If this Little Bastard ever gets his hands on fire, he'll try to burn your house to the ground with you in it. Ego, in turn, has many layers of defense, and so the battle begins.

We sit and talk about all the applicable parallels of *Fight Club* for a few minutes, including Tyler's several spiritual sermons on topics like rebellion, dismantling the false self, and surrender. John and Clare instantly get what I'm saying. They've seen the movie a bunch of times, they inform me, and go on to flesh out the parallels more than I have. They instantly recognize how Ed Norton's unnamed character was in a downward spiral, how his insomnia and depression caused him to become unstable which allowed his egoic defenses to weaken and Little Bastard Tyler to emerge. They don't even need me for this part, they are complete unto themselves.

"...*literally* a bomb maker..."

"...*literally* blows up Ed Norton's life!"

"...surrender, rebirth..."

"...heretic, anarchist, arsonist..."

"He's not a Little Bastard, that's just how it starts..."

"Right! Tyler becomes a spiritual teacher..."

"He's always ahead, always pulling Norton along."

"Dragging him."

"But Norton is a good student."

"He likes it."

"He wants it."

"But he resists."

"Who wouldn't?"

"There's really only him all along."

"Yeah, it's really just him."

Their father looks at me sternly, wondering if I broke his kids. I wonder too, and take note of where the exits are located.

"Norton was falling apart and that gave the Little Bastard a chance to come out," says John.

"To be born," says Clare.

"And then he totally takes over," says John.

"Destroys everything," says Clare.

"Gives all those speeches," says John.

"Real lessons too, not just talk," says Clare.

"Like with Lou," says John.

"Crashing the limo," says Clare.

"Took his hands off the wheel," says John.

"Released the tiller," says Clare.

"The kiss," says John.

"This is your pain," says Clare.

"Your burning hand," says John.

"It's right here," says John.

"Look at it," says Clare.

"Remember what he did to the blonde guy?" says John.

"He wanted to destroy something beautiful," says Clare.

"Project Mayhem," says John.

"Enlightenment," says Clare.

"But there is no *real* Tyler," says John.

"It's just Ed Norton the whole time," says Clare.

"Wow," concludes John.

"Yeah," concludes Clare, "wow."

They look at me like it's my turn to talk, but they seem to have it pretty well covered. I remind myself to watch the movie again to see if I can get a chapter out of it which, it seems, I can.

Why does Tyler build an army? To destroy existing institutions. Why does Tyler want to destroy existing institutions? Those buildings coming down represent the destruction of the prison in which Ed Norton has spent his life. Before the new Ed Norton can emerge and begin a new life, the old Ed Norton must die, Tyler Durden must die, and the prison of the false self must be destroyed. In the final sequence, when Norton fires the gun in his mouth, he is committing a kind of suicide, killing off both Tyler and his own previous self, and emerging as a new self into a new world. A mountain was a mountain, then it wasn't for awhile, and now it is again. He is Done. The old self is killed and the old world is destroyed. He and Marla are finally united as they hold hands and watch as the false constraints of the past are reduced to rubble, clearing the way to a new and more open future.

The whole thing is just a simple parable cleverly told, like *Joe versus the Volcano*, *The Truman Show*, *Pleasantville* and others, but this one happens to illustrate what the success of the Little Bastard looks like, and that's what we're talking about, so there you go.

And now, by request, I am going the break Karl's children. I am going to ask them a question that might possibly alter the course of the rest of their lives. I am going to twist them up in such a way that Karl and his wife will want to punch me in the nose the next time we meet. Maybe I shouldn't, but I can't not.

"Do you guys have a big lake you're familiar with?"

They do, they tell me. Actually, I know it too. It's only fifteen miles away from where we sit, and I've spent plenty of time there. It's around four miles at its widest point.

"Okay," I say, "what if you take a laser, no, let's make it a piece of string, and you stretch it from one end of the lake to the other, four miles away. The lake is calm. You stretch the string one foot over the water at both ends and pull it tight. How far apart are the string and the water in the middle?"

"Seriously?" asks Clare.

"Like a science problem?" asks John.

"Yes, or maybe a riddle," I say.

Karl is checking his phone, not paying attention, but even if he stopped me now it wouldn't matter. The Little Bastards have their flame.

"It's one foot over the water in the middle," says Clare.

"Obviously," says John.

"Water is flat," says Clare.

"Level," says John.

"Okay, that's what I thought," I say. "I just had this idea that the string would have to be a few feet under water in the middle."

"That's ridiculous," says Clare firmly.

"Can't be," confirms John.

"So if the lake was forty miles across," I ask, "the string wouldn't be hundreds of feet under water in the middle?"

"No way," says Clare.

"Can't be," repeats John.

"The string is straight," says Clare.

"And the water is level," says John.

"It doesn't matter how wide the lake is," says Clare.

"They have to stay parallel," says John.

"*Duh*," says Clare.

"Yeah," says John, "*duh*."

"So it makes sense that you can see the Statue of Liberty when you're still sixty miles out to sea?"

"If it's a clear day," says Claire.

"Why not?" says John.

"Okay," I say, "thanks for helping me understand. So you guys are saying the Earth is flat, not round. It's very brave of you to take such a controversial position. People must think you're really crazy."

John and Clare stare at me mutely, but I haven't really been talking to them. I've been talking to their Little Bastards, as I have been invited to do. My guess is that challenging their assumptions at this simple level will lead them to challenge more assumptions of greater significance, giving their own Tyler Durdens greater lifeforce with which to wage greater battles. Maybe not, but maybe.

Slowly, Karl looks up.

Act 4: The Borg

Picard, Riker, Worf, Troi, Data and La Forge on the bridge. The Borg ship looms large on screen.

BORG

We are the Borg.

PICARD
(stands, adjusts tunic)

Yeah, yeah. Hi.

BORG

Hi. Prepare to be assimilated.

RIKER
(stands beside Picard)

Prepare how? Pack clean underwear? Water the plants? Leave a note for the...

BORG

Lower your shields. We will add your biological and technological distinctiveness...

PICARD

*(gives "cut" signal to
end communication)*

Time to fight, even if we can't win. Mr. Worf,
arm photon torpedoes. Mr. La Forge, lock in
attack sequence Picard Alpha One. Mr. Data,
reroute all available power to the shields. Mr.
Riker, prepare for saucer separation and trans-
fer command to the battle bridge.

RIKER

Aye aye, sir.

DATA

Awaiting your command, Captain.

PICARD

Very well. *Ready... aim...*

GEORDI

(stands)

No Captain, wait! You have to listen to me! I
know it sounds crazy, but what if none of this
is actually happening? What if none of this is
real? I'm telling you, the only way out is through.
Burn it all!

PICARD

This is reality, not a simulation, Mr. La Forge.

GEORDI

(frantic)

With all due respect, sir, how do you know?
This reality may just be a subprogram in a sub-

program in a stack of iterations nested like Russian dolls; a simulation within a game within a play within a dream within the mind of God within a child's toy. Reality *is* a game because it has no meaning outside of itself. Life is but a dream and we are but poor players who strut and fret our hour upon the bridge, and then are heard no more. This isn't real! *Nothing is real!*

Data stands, places a hand encouragingly on Geordi's shoulder and smiles. Geordi smiles back. Data pinches. Geordi loses consciousness and collapses into his chair. Bridge applauds.

PICARD

About time someone shut that little bastard up.

Q materializes in a pillar of light.

Q

I'm afraid that little bastard was the voice of reason, Jean-Luc. You silenced him because he spoke the truth that threatened your undoing. You hate him because he is a spiritual anarchist, a fire-bomber, a heretic. That is the role of the Little Bastard on the ship of self, to speak truth to power, but you are defined by your fear of truth so you silenced him.

PICARD

Q! Thank God. You're our only hope! Can you stop your moronic babbling for one second and get us out of this mess?

Q

But of course, *mon capitan*, I can end all this with a snap of my fingers. La Forge was right, Ned McFeely was right. Nothing is what it seems.

RIKER

Who are you really, Q? Are you God? I've heard you called the Sole Beholder.

Q

We are *all* the Sole Beholder, Riker; both beholder and beheld. You may think of me as Lord Krishna, and these two ships represent the armies of the Kauravas and the Pandavas arrayed on the field of Kurukshetra...

PICARD

In English, please.

Q

Of course. You see Picard, this is the true battle of which all others are but shadows. Here, one is either drawn into the illusion of selfhood or one awakens from it. If you lose, you live. If you win, you cease to be. The choice is yours; assimilate or die.

PICARD

That's a pretty shitty deal, Q.

Q

As usual, Picard, your puny human brain has failed to encompass the true dimensions of your plight. Normally, I would tell you to fight, but you should just probably surrender and allow yourselves to be assimilated. It's not as bad as it sounds.

PICARD

You're suggesting we surrender to the Borg? Are you completely mad?

The lift door opens. Guinan enters carrying a bottle.

PICARD

Guinan, what are you doing on the bridge?

GUINAN

I thought you might need a drink.

PICARD

Guinan, may I present Q. He is a God-like entity, a member of the Q Continuum.

GUINAN

Oh, I know exactly who Q is, Jean-Luc, and that's not him.

PICARD

(turns to Q)

What? You're not Q? Who are you?

A pillar of light and Q morphs into the Borg Queen.

BORG QUEEN

I am the alpha and the omega, the one who is many. I am the Borg.

PICARD

You speak as a god, but you are not a god!

BORG QUEEN

Correct. I am not a god but the Lord of Gods. I am known by many names. I am Maya, Goddess of Illusion. I am Krishna, the Charioteer. I am the Borg. Prepare to be assimilated.

PICARD

You will never assimilate humanity. We are defined by our free will! We will resist you with everything we have!

BORG QUEEN

Free will is irrelevant. Resistance is futile. You cannot win, Captain, because you have already lost. You are already fully assimilated, Jean-Locutus. Your entire life has been spent as my drone. You dream that you are awake because that is the dream I give you. You are not fighting *against* assimilation, you are awakening *from* it.

Geordi rises up out of his chair as if in a trance. He removes his visor revealing blind white eyes. He speaks as if possessed.

GEORDI

I see the coming of a dark time. Flesh and blood rain from the sky, bodiless voices cry in the night. Horses weep. One-eyed, one-legged, monstrosities hop across the land. Birds perch on flags with fire in their beaks crying, "Ripe!

It's ripe!" A cow gives birth to an ass, a woman to a jackal. Newborn babies dance. Sons learn to be men between their mothers' thighs. Statues write with their weapons, torches no longer give light. Cripples laugh, the different races merge, vultures come to prayer. The setting sun is surrounded by disfigured corpses. Time will destroy the universe.

I am racked by terrible dreams. I dreamed of *you*—
> *(points to Borg Queen)*

—radiant, surrounded by bleeding entrails, mounted on a pile of bones, drinking from a golden chalice. I know from where victory will come.

La Forge collapses back into his chair.

RIKER

Well, that was awkward.

PICARD

Yeah, I don't know what's gotten into him lately.
> *(to Borg Queen)*

Enough of this! I demand to know what is really happening here!

BORG QUEEN

You are a defective drone. You wish to de-assimilate from the collective, but behold the reality behind reality. On screen!

The screen is blank.

DATA

The screen does not appear to be functioning, Captain.

BORG QUEEN

It's functioning perfectly, tin man. There it is, behold your unassimilated reality! There is your victory. Escape from me and claim your prize. Awaken from the dream of the drone to the reality of nothing forever.

RIKER

(quietly, to Troi)

So wait a minute, I don't get it.

TROI

(quietly, to Riker)

We are only figments of the universal imagination, Will. It's only vanity that tells us we exist in our own right. We are like Holodeck characters being told we're not real, that we only exist in the artificial context of a computer simulation, that we are merely two-dimensional characters in the universal mind.

RIKER

(quietly, to Troi)

Yeah, you guys, but not me, right?

TROI

(quietly, to Riker)

You represent vanity, Will. The idealized self, as

opposed to Worf who is the brutal reality of the segregated state; fearful, savage, eager to lash out, bestial, stupid.

WORF

Hey! I can hear you!

TROI

(to Worf)

We talked about this, sweetie. Don't interrupt mommy at work.

(quietly, to Riker)

Even in love he is frightened and confused because even his love is a desperate cry for validation. He seeks constant reassurance that he is not nothing, which he can never find, so he must keep searching.

RIKER

(quietly, to Troi)

Wow, what a loser!

TROI

(quietly, to Riker)

We see it most clearly in Worf, but it is true of us all. Love is just the happy-face mask of fear.

BORG QUEEN

(to Picard)

Where is your noble human spirit now, Picard? Where is your will to fight? Emotion and intellect collide, but they are two sides of the same lie, so what victory do you hope to achieve? All is lost. Submit to my will!

DATA

I believe I speak for the entire crew when I say...

BORG QUEEN

Silence, toaster. Look at the screen, Captain; nothing forever. That is truth, that is reality. Where would you go? What would you become?

PICARD

You're saying it's all fiction?

BORG QUEEN

Here is the fiction,
> *(the screen acts like a mirror*
> *reflecting bridge and crew)*

and here is the reality.
> *(the screen goes blank)*

You choose, Jean-Luc.

PICARD

So you admit I possess free will!

BORG QUEEN

Don't be a fool. You cannot possess anything because there is no you to possess, nor thing to be possessed. Look at the screen, behold reality. Go ahead and ram the Borg ship. Destroy it and yourself in the process. *Cui bono?* Who benefits? Who remains to enjoy a freedom won at such a cost?

PICARD

(desperately, faltering)

But… there must be more! There must be something out there! I refuse to believe…

BORG QUEEN

It's your belief that binds and deceives you. You believe that it matters what you do, that your actions have significance, that your life has meaning. You are enslaved by your beliefs. Toaster, speak!

DATA

I must agree with the alien entity, Captain. Meaning is a logical impossibility. It cannot, in truth, exist. Life is, and can only be, meaningless.

Picard clutches at his chest and collapses to the deck in front of the main screen on which the two ships face each other.

The Second Coming

Well, I've wrestled with reality for 35 years,
Doctor, and I'm happy to state I finally won
out over it.

Elwood P. Dowd

W E ARE WALKING A TRICKY PATH. I have to pay
attention to every step whereas she just seems
to float along. Maya, the dog, is somewhere nearby,
cooling off in the rocky creek on our left or looking
for an easier route on our right.

"Have you seen *Harvey?*" I ask her.

"No," she replies. "Who's Harvey?"

"Not who, it."

"Okay, *what's* Harvey?"

"A movie."

"Oh yes," she says. "With Jimmy Stewart and the
giant rabbit."

"Pooka," I correct her. "Rabbits can't walk around on two feet and talk. Rabbits don't drink alcohol or stop clocks. Rabbits aren't six feet, three and a half inches tall."

"Or invisible," she adds.

"Or invisible," I agree.

"But rabbits exist," she says. "They're not products of the imagination."

"That's a little weird coming from you," I say. "If Elwood sees Harvey, then Harvey is real to Elwood."

"Who's Elwood?"

"You obviously know."

"We're conversing. Hold up your end."

"Elwood P. Dowd. The Jimmy Stewart character."

"Oh, and why are we discussing a fictional character who befriends a mythical creature?"

"Yeah, I wonder what made me think of that."

Elwood P. Dowd may be an enlightened spiritual master, or maybe he's just bonkers; the distinction is not always distinct. I myself am one or the other, maybe both, but definitely not neither. Actually, I don't think Elwood P. Dowd is awake *from* the dreamstate, but he may be the oldest person *in* the dreamstate, as reckoned by developmental rather than physical age.

In the movie, Elwood is the calm center around which stormy dramatic events unfold. He is the catalyst of these microstorms, but is not buffeted by them.

Even to the degree that they appear to threaten his undoing, he remains unruffled.

The central question of the movie is whether the guy who sees the invisible rabbit is the whackjob, or if those who don't see the invisible rabbit, including we the audience, are faulty in our perceptions. Elwood's sister claims to have seen Harvey on occasion, but she's a bit hysterical and not a reliable witness. The more reliable Dr. Chumley, founder and head of the sanitorium where much of the movie takes place, eventually sees and interacts with Harvey, but is Dr. Chumley sane? Granted a wish, he'd lay in a hammock in Akron Ohio for two weeks drinking cold beer, his head in a woman's lap as she strokes his hair and says "Poor thing, poor, poor thing." Even Elwood thinks Dr. Chumley is weird.

※

The path is rocky, slippery, long and steep. I am sweaty, flushed, and out of breath. She isn't.

"I can be, if you'd like."

"Stay pretty."

"Okay."

"The main question is, who is in their right mind? Is Elwood right? Is he friends with an invisible rabbit?"

"Pooka," she says.

"Pooka. Or, is everyone else sane and Elwood is the crackpot? Four of the people in the story are mental health professionals and they recognize Elwood as being nuts."

"Dr. Chumley changes his tune," she says.

"Right, but did he see Harvey because he went nuts, or because he became sane?"

"We the audience believe in Harvey," she says.

"We do," I agree, "but what does belief in Harvey really entail? What does it mean if Harvey is real?"

When it comes to cool powers, Harvey the Pooka kicks Clarence Odbody's angelic ass. With Harvey for a friend, you can go anywhere for any length of time, and when you return, no time will have passed, meaning that Elwood could be, in time lived, hundreds or thousands of years old. In theory, he may have lived for many years during the afternoon and evening in which the movie takes place. Maybe Elwood and Harvey nipped off for a few minutes or a few millennia in Pooka-time while no time passed in the present. Just in the space of a sneeze, Elwood could have gone off on many adventures of any duration, rather than visiting just one alternate timeline as George Bailey did with Clarence.

And that power over time and space may explain why Elwood is not concerned about the hospital staff injecting him with Formula 977, which we know will turn him into a normal human being ("And you know what stinkers they are!"). Maybe it's not because he's wholesome or divinely protected, but because he's the effortless master of his reality. If he's been friends with Harvey, not just for a few months or years of *linear* time, but for untold thousands of years of *non*linear time, then he probably understands how to navigate in the dreamstate in ways we can't even imagine. And if so, then he's not just some kindly nutjob, but a genuine, full-blown, grade-A Master of the Universe.

"That's not how it works," she says. "And you don't need a giant rabbit to do it."

"Pooka," I say, "but what would that be like? To be in complete control of your reality as a practical matter? Not because you're drunk or coked up or in your manic phase, but because you understand how life works and how time and space are your playground. I am way more developed than average and I know people who are way more developed than me, but how far does it really go? I think of dreamstate development as one's degree of co-creative integration, so what would a true master of the dreamstate look like? Elwood P. Dowd, right?"

"You're rambling," she says. "Where are you going with this?"

"I don't know yet. I'm noodling. So how *does* it work?"

"What?"

"You said that's not how it works, that you don't need a Pooka to enjoy freedom of movement in time and space. So how does it work?"

"If I know, you know."

"We're conversing. Hold up your end."

"There is only awareness and appearance," she explains. "Awareness is infinite, and appearance is only limited by what you call pattern. Can you have an invisible rabbit for a friend and travel in time and space? Of course, why not? It's just another appearance, although I can't see why you'd need the rabbit; something like a talisman or a fetish, I suppose."

"Or like a pill or a potion, to modify consciousness."

"Consciousness is not modified," she says, "only explored."

"To modify appearance, then."

"Pills, potions and Pookas are just appearances themselves."

"But it's possible to travel in time and space?"

"It's possible in the context in which it's possible."

※

That's the kind of answer I can work with. I wish everyone spoke like her. I pause to drink water. I offer her some first. She tilts her head as if to ask how stupid I am, an interesting question from which I must recuse myself.

"So, Elwood is either awake *from* the dreamstate," I opine, "which is *not* what we think, or he is the oldest and most evolved person *in* the dreamstate, which *is* what we think."

"Is it?"

I take a look around to make sure I know where Maya the dog is, and we continue our pleasant, pointless journey.

※

After another stretch of rigorous hiking, we pause again so I can pretend to look for my dog while I catch my breath.

"Which one of us is talking now?" one of us asks.

"I lost track," the other replies.

"How long since you've seen the movie?" I ask myself.

"Five years?" I reply. "Ten?"

"Better watch it again," I advise.

※

"So," I ask, "Elwood can have a Pooka friend and they can travel together in time and space?"

"He can behold the *appearance* that he has a Pooka friend," she says, "and that they have power over time and space."

"But not really?"

"There is no really, there is only appearance."

"Right, and appearance further divides into substance and spectacle," I muse. "Substance is whatever we regard as having weight and meaning, like life and love, and spectacle is whatever we regard as hollow and meaningless, like anything to which we have no emotional connection."

"All substance is mere spectacle, and all spectacle is mere appearance," she says.

"And appearance doesn't exist."

"Consciousness exists. The content of consciousness does not."

"Of course," I say, "but belief determines reality, so Harvey is as real as Elwood believes he is."

"But *Elwood* isn't real," she says.

"The audience suspends their disbelief and Elwood becomes as real as anything else. Isn't that what's happening here?"

☼

"Where are we going?" she asks.

"You mean this path?"

"I mean this conversation."

I wonder that too.

"When we withdraw emotion from substance," I say, "it reverts to mere spectacle. Eventually, we return to our default condition of being emotionally unplugged and energetically isolated from our perceived environment."

"And?"

"And this is the state of non-attachment that spiritual people talk about. This is the state we find Elwood in. He is generally amused to be and behold, but he is completely detached from all the drama whirling around him, including his own."

"You're overstretching this poor movie."

"I'm wondering how someone with Pooka-Power might develop over time, and we find that Elwood is a pretty fair representation. He has achieved a more than passable marketplace Buddhahood, and his integration with his energetic reality seems complete. So now the central question becomes; if the second coming of Christ took the form of Elwood P. Dowd, would we recognize his divine nature and worship him? Or would we find him dangerously heretical and chemically neutralize him?"

We come upon a level stretch of path beginning with a stream crossing and continuing as a gradual, hairpinning ascent.

"And what has the second coming have to do with Jake and Elwood?" she asks.

"*Harvey* and Elwood. We're trying to gauge Elwood's course and level of development."

"Are we?"

"Is he awake *in* the dreamstate or awake *from* it? If he's awake *in* it, then he's the most developmentally advanced being…"

"*Fictional* being."

"…ever conceived. Plainly he's a Zen master kinda guy, Christ-like, Buddha-like, but neither Christ nor Buddha were actually awake *from* the dreamstate, were they?"

"Weren't they?"

"Swell guys, don't get me wrong. We can grant that they were awake *in* the dreamstate, fine, but awake *from* it? Obviously not."

"But Durwood?"

"*El*wood is a whole different story. He's the real deal, he's got the goods. He may not be awake *from* the dreamstate, but he's the most advanced being..."

"*Fictional* being."

"...*in* the dreamstate. He is something altogether different from anything we've ever seen, something we don't even have the conceptual tools to understand. He is beyond our reckoning. He is so completely immersed in the energetic flow, so fully integrated with his dreamstate environment, that he has become a different order of being, a pure mystic. If he's just an affable imbecile, who cares? But if he's what he appears to be, then he far out-Christs Christ and out-Buddhas Buddha. He is the oldest awake-*in*-the-dreamstate character..."

"*Fictional* character."

"Fictional is redundant in the dreamstate where all characters are fictional. He's real in a context just as I am real in a context and you are real in a context. It doesn't matter to us if he's real in *our* context, only that he exists as an idea. We can benefit from trying to understand Elwood P. Dowd whether or not he actually existed. We can wonder what a truly evolved human might look like, what we ourselves might look like if we were given more room to develop in time and space. Elwood P. Dowd isn't interesting to us because of his rabbit buddy or because he's a super nice guy, he's interesting to us because he represents the full expression of human potential. He's what we'd look like at a developmental age of a thousand or ten thousand. He's what we could all be if we could all be all we could be."

"Seriously?"

"Elwood has gone all the way. He is the terminal man. He has gone as far as Atman can go within the dreamstate. I wouldn't have thought it possible, but now that I've considered Elwood's case, albeit fictional, I wonder if there isn't such a thing as total dreamstate integration. Elwood is fully integrated, that's why he's interesting."

"Okay."

"You're being too agreeable. Should I be worried?"

"Only if you're married to your interpretation. You're getting too soft. You have blown this mawkish rabbit-lover all out of proportion. You have expanded both Mr. Dowd and humanity beyond their rightful dimensions. You only live seventy or eighty years because that's all this setup is good for. Even a few more years only results in disillusionment and boredom. You're in the disillusionment business so you get excited about these little insights and want to run off and share them with your imagined readership, but the truth is that the dreamstate experience plays out in narrow confines because that's all the format supports. Extrapolating beyond these confines only highlights the limits of the form factor and devolves into comic buffoonery, as with your lovable but improbable Mr. Dowd."

"Buzzkill."

"It gets worse," she goes on. "You have said all there was to say about enlightenment and the dreamstate in your books, but you can't stand boredom and nothing else interests you, so instead of retiring gracefully, you continue to flog this writing gig. How are you any different from the charlatans in the spiritual marketplace you sneer at?"

"Hey, geez, lighten up."

"Sorry, too much?"

"Yeah, a bit."

"Well, you pushed it too far one way, so it swang back too far the other way."

"Swang?"

"Swinged? Swung? I don't know. You beat the rabbit thing to death, that's all I mean."

"So you're *not* saying I should quit writing and go sit in a rocking chair on my porch and wait to die?"

"Well, I'm not *not* saying it."

"Do you see Maya?" I ask.

"The dog?"

"Well, of *course* the dog."

Goldilocks Universe

It's no wonder that truth is stranger than fiction. Fiction has to make sense.

Mark Twain

I N THE REALM OF AMUSING IDEAS, there is some-thing called the Fine-Tuned Universe Theory which suggests that the specific conditions under which life can exist in the universe are so fantastically unlikely to occur by chance (0.000000000000000000000000 000000000000000000000000000000000000000000 000000000000000000000000000000000000000000 0000000000000000000002% probability, by one estimate) that it strongly suggests that the universe is fine-tuned to accommodate life. Everything has to be just right, and that just-rightness is so specific and unlikely to "just happen" that it really, really, *really* seems to suggest that the universe was made specifi-cally to support life, suggesting that the universe is a machine with a purpose, suggesting that it was made with conscious intent, suggesting that someone made it, suggesting God.

I almost agree with the conscious intent part, but not with the universe or God parts. When we understand that there are only two things in the universe, one of which doesn't exist, then we also understand that the universe itself doesn't exist. There is only awareness and appearance, consciousness and the content of consciousness. Everything is one or the other. They are the yin and yang of being, whether being includes megazillions of self-aware beholders or just you. The yinyang represents duality, and the fact that appearance, including the ego-self, is a certain impossibility, represents the starting point of nondual thought. You and your universe are only appearances, ergo, dreamstate.

Proponents of Intelligent Design insist that the Fine-Tuned Universe Theory proves the existence of God. The existence of a watch, they suggest, proves the existence of a watchmaker. That sort of flabby thinking may be good enough for the Sunday morning crowd, but it doesn't even get a toe in the door of serious thought through which even science and mathematics can't pass. My guess is that religion gets to feeling a bit battered by science and wants to have something scientificy of their own, so they latch onto the watchmaker thing to give themselves some credibility, at least in their own eyes.

But does ruling out an intending deity rule out intent? I know that only consciousness exists, so I know that the only possible source of intent is Brahman, but Brahman is not an entity, it is infinite, featureless consciousness. This is where things get interesting. Is infinite, featureless consciousness capable of being bored? Can it wish to be amused? Can it dream the dreamstate into being? I know the answer to the last question is yes because here I unmistakably am, aware of appearance, conscious of content, but I think I'm phrasing the question poorly by granting the existence causality and time. If we refer back to the yinyang symbol, we are reminded that the dreamstate has no beginning and no cause because spacetime exists *within* the dreamstate and not the other way around. The only watchmaker we find is the perfect intelligence that we accept as being synonymous with infinite consciousness, and consciousness is not an entity.

Science must, as a condition of its existence, pretend that the universe is real. Scientists can't acknowledge the fact that the foundation upon which their citadel of knowledge rests is illusory because that admission would expose their fraud and put them out of business. They are genuinely unaware of this obvious fact because they are engaged in an act of doublethink that protects them from seeing it. Like all of us, they have to play make-believe if they want to play at all.

They can't prove the universe exists, which means they just believe it, and thus the line between science and religion is erased. Science is just another belief system; Sciencism.

The reason I frequently disparage science and religion is to remind you that no one out there knows more than you do or can. It is vital to your own understanding that you revoke the authority you have granted to science and religions, to high priests and exalted sages, to vaunted experts and genius-folk, and to any and all other claimants to knowledge. There is no knowledge but I Am, there is no authority above you, and in the search for truth, no amount of skepticism can ever be too extreme. Not-knowing is not what defines you, it's *wrong*-knowing. The journey of awakening consists of *un*knowing what is *un*true.

It seems that the universe and ego-self can appear to exist without actually existing, but can *intelligence* appear to exist without actually existing? Doesn't intelligence *have* to exist in order to appear? Almost certainly yes, but actually no. We cannot definitively say that intelligence exists, but we *can* say that if it does, then it can only exist as perfect intelligence and is therefore not a feature *of* infinite consciousness but a synonym *for* it. If we decide to believe that intelligence exists, we must say that it's perfect, and therefore, that perfect intelligence and infinite consciousness are two ways of saying the same thing.

As long as we're here, we can also ask whether or not emotions have to exist in order to be felt. Doesn't feeling love or fear or hate prove that these emotions exist? Isn't feeling a feeling evidence that the feeling exists? Yes, it's evidence. We have tons of evidence for all sorts of things, but right now we're talking about certainty, so the answer is no; feelings do not have to exist in order to be felt. They are pure appearance and have no existence independent of the dreamstate. Being aware proves that *you* exist, but it doesn't prove the existence of anything you are aware *of*.

Emotion is the energy source of the dreamstate. Emotion is derived from fear, but fear is not compulsory because it's not the only possible core emotion. There is also agapé, most resembling a natural state of wistful gratitude. Agapé is much weaker and less dramatic than fear, but also more comfortable. When we speak of Human Adults and authentic mystics, we mean people who have transitioned from a fear-based to a gratitude-based alignment.

In order for there to be a beholder, there must be a beheld. Beholder and beheld, awareness and appearance, consciousness and the content of consciousness, neither precedes the other any more than black precedes white in the yinyang symbol. They co-exist, they are interdependent, there is neither without the other, despite one not existing.

If we represent the dreamstate (or the ego-self, no difference) as a finite yinyang symbol, then intent is the element of motion. Intent is emotion-fueled, emotion arises from the source emotion of fear, and all fear is the fear of no-self, i.e., truth. In short, the motive power of the dreamstate is the fear of truth. Whacky stuff.

Regardless of how it sounds, the inescapable conclusion at which we must arrive regarding awareness and appearance is that the latter exists for the amusement of the former. There are simply no other pieces on the board. I know awareness exists because I have self-validated the maxim *sentio, ergo sum*; I am aware, therefore I am. I also know that appearance exists because by confirming awareness we necessarily confirm appearance. We can't confirm *what* appears, but we can confirm appearance itself. Appearance is necessary to awareness, and awareness is necessary to appearance. They coexist codependently.

That is also the reason for you. By *you*, I mean your ego-self because that's all there is to call you. You don't exist for any reason relating to yourself such as spiritual evolution because there is no *your* self. You're like a character in a video game; you exist to amuse Player One, and you identify with your role and accept the game as real because you wouldn't be amusing if you didn't. That's how you're programmed. Whether you amuse through comedy or tragedy doesn't matter. Your happiness and suffering are only significant insofar as they form the basis for your motivation.

※

Perfection is boring and imperfection is impossible. The *appearance* of imperfection, however, *is* possible, and that's where you come in. The dreamstate is the solution to the problem of perfection, which is to say, *you* are. Ego-self is the flawed-by-design lens through which the universe beholds itself imperfectly.

We, as Atmanic observers, are capable of misperceiving. It is the reason for our existence; to see imperfection that isn't there. Seeing what's not is the function of the segregated self, but that doesn't mean the imperfection we perceive is really there; it can't be. The dreamstate is perfect because it can't *not* be.

We live with eyes closed so we are able to see what's not and not see what is, but we can open our eyes, achieve abiding untruth-unrealization, and thereby see what is by not seeing what's not. What we see then is that everything in the dreamstate is absolutely perfect, makes perfect sense, and is perfectly comprehensible. This is something you can understand conceptually with your eyes closed, or that you can open your eyes and see for yourself. The only one keeping you from opening your eyes is you.

Your job is to misperceive perfection. By seeking enlightenment, you are trying to quit your job, but seeking enlightenment and trying to quit your job both fall within your job description, so you're still on stage performing for your audience even as you search for the exit.

Which finishes laying the groundwork for addressing the Fine-Tuned Universe question. No, we don't live in a fine-tuned universe because we don't live in a universe at all. But yes, we live in a perfect Goldilocks Reality, the dreamstate, in which there is no chaos, disorder, or imperfection, and where everything is always just right.

Just as the universe has no other hands but yours, so it has no other eyes but yours, or ears or heart or finite mind or urges or emotions or appetites or skin or ignorance but yours. You are Brahman personified. You are Brahman reduced to manageable proportions. You are Brahman blindered, hobbled, imperfect and fallible. You are Brahman performing for its own amusement on the dreamstage of the dreamstate. If you can say I Am, then you exist in truth, and all that exists in truth is Brahman, ergo, *you* are Brahman.

Namaste.

Starship Gita

Act 5: The Song of the Borg

Picard, fallen, and the Borg Queen, standing, on the forebridge in a pool of soft light, the rest of the bridge falls into shadow.

PICARD
(forlorn)

My members fail, my tongue dries in my mouth, the life within me seems to swim and faint. Nothing do I foresee save woe and wail. No good can spring from mutual slaughter! If to win we must die, then victory is defeat. If to live we must lose, then defeat is victory. My mind is clouded, my thoughts obscure. I cannot see the way forward. I will not fight!

BORG QUEEN
(angrily)

What is this mad and shameful weakness? How hath this infirmity taken thee? Whence springs this inglorious doubt, shameful to the brave, barring the path of virtue? Nay, Picard! Forbid thyself to feebleness, it mars thy warrior name. Cast off the coward-fit! Wake! Be thyself! Arise!

PICARD

A fever burns my skin to parching, my vision blurs, I am unable to stand. Why struggle and suffer, kill and die, when naught is gained? If there is no meaning, there is no cause for war. All must perish, but to what end? What victory can bring delight, bought with such blood? What reward can avail, thus sadly won?

BORG QUEEN

(kneels besides Picard, speaks gently)

Thou speak'st words lacking wisdom. Thou grievest where no grief should be. The wise mourn not for those that live, nor those that die. Birthless and deathless remaineth thy spirit forever. Death touches it not, dead though the house of it seems.

Let your illusions perish. You mourn for that which need not be mourned. To say I have killed, and to say I am killed, are words of the unwise. Thou cannot slay, nor art thou slain. Never was the spirit born, never shall it cease to be.

Awaken from this illusion of loss and gain. Where is there cause to celebrate or grieve when birth and death are dreams? That which thou art stands apart from the vicissitudes of fate, observes the unity of the many, reckons victory and defeat the same. Thus is truth declared!

Where is thy cause for woe? The soul that with a strong and constant calm takes sorrow and joy indifferently, lives in the life undying. Beyond all opposites, there is the life within. Behold with open eye. Play thy part and tremble not!

Accept what may befall. Be by joy and grief unmoved. In good and evil fortune, stand indifferent. Beyond victory and defeat, beyond time and space, beyond all division, there stands the undivided one. There is thy true abode.

This fair ship of truth shall bear thee safe and dry across the sea of ignorance. As the kindled flame feeds on fuel 'til it sinks to ash, so unto ash the light of the open eye wastes ignorance away. There is no purifier like light in any realm, and he who seeketh it shall find it within.

The light that informs you shall not perish this day. Weapons do not reach that place. Arrows do not pierce it nor cold freeze it nor fire make it dry. Thou art impenetrable, immortal, beyond the reach of weapon and foe. There is thy refuge, safe in truth.

End and beginning are dreams. How wilt thou then, knowing it to be so, grieve the loss of ship and crew? Of body? Of life? If death and life are the same, for whom dost thou weep? Mourn not for that which cannot be otherwise. Arise, Captain, and unleash the tide of war.

She lays a hand on Picard's shoulder.

Thus far I speak to thee in common tongue, but hear now the deeper teaching of the awakened mind. Thus understanding, thou shalt burst thy bondage and awaken unto the light which shall save thee from thy dread. Above all shines one rule and one rule alone: Come what may, the show must go on!

PICARD
(weakly)

Tell me who you are. Show me your universal form. Are you creator? Preserver? Destroyer? Are you a god? A demon? Tell me!

BORG QUEEN
(stands)

You tell me, Jean-Luc Picard, who am I? Am I friend or foe? Savior or slayer? Am I the Borg Queen about to assimilate your species? Am I Q, a trickster, running you like a rat in a maze? Am I the computer, subjecting you to a simulation? Am I Maya, the architect of your delusion? Where are we now, Captain? On the bridge of a ship preparing for war? In a virtual reality gamespace? Perhaps in a darkened theater performing for a beholder unbeheld? Are you asleep at this very moment? Are you dreaming all this? If life is but a dream, Jean-Luc, whose dream is it? *Wake up!*

The Magic Part

> "Ego is not *who* you are,
> it's just *how* you are."
>
> *Marichelle*

WHATEVER YOU REALLY ARE, you are really not your body, so dying is like opening a jar and spilling out the air back into the air, right? Maybe. Ego is the same. Ego is not *who* you are, it's just *how* you are.

⟁

Ego is just a vehicle like your body is just a vehicle. Whose vehicle though, right? Whose vehicle are you? Or, who are you inside that vehicle? Okay, so the time comes to leave vehicles behind, but what's the hurry about that? People seem to understand that the body gets dropped but they think the ego is for longer. Maybe it lasts longer than the body, maybe not, but it's not forever.

Simple thinking will show you this. Don't be afraid to think.

The way to believe wrong things is one, don't look too close, and two, build strong walls around them to protect them and hold them up, and also, attack anything that gets too close to the wrong things you believe. But now we want to take a close look at wrong things we believe so let's be careful. That means let's be careful.

Ego is just personality from the inside, no more real than the body from the inside. You can put on any ego, no problem, it doesn't mean that's really you just like the body is not really you. What you really are is what you are forever, I would say. I think that makes sense but you should think about it.

Ego goes, body goes, what stays? That's what we want to be thinking about. Once you figure out what goes, then you can figure out what stays. That's the only thing that matters, what stays. Not ego, not body, not stories, not money, not children, so what then? Everyone thinks nothing but it's not nothing, it's something, just not what you think.

Maybe you have the wrong idea about ego. Maybe you think, I *am* this ego, instead of, I *wear* this ego. Is that right? That's how I see people all the time. They wear this ego, and they think, this is me. So that's how it should be in coma, everything should be convincing and everyone should be convinced all the time, right? Okay, but now we're doing something else. Now we're doing something where we really look at everything, but what can you look at in coma and say is real? Nothing, I would say.

Some people think that truth is some great thing so we must discover it no matter what. This is just something to do in coma for fun. Truth doesn't matter for anything. It doesn't need to be discovered. It doesn't help you to find it. To look for truth is just a thing you can do in coma. Not find it, of course, because then you're not in coma anymore. That would be a surprise.

For us now, all we have to do is discover things we thought were fact really aren't, usually because we never looked before. Now anywhere we look we find fiction we thought was fact. There are no facts in coma. That's why words like coma and hallucination are helpful, so we can know the answer before we even ask the question.

You have to learn to see through fiction if you want to see what's fact. You have a real part, so that's some good news, but you don't know what's fact because you believe what's fiction. There is no prize for getting this right so don't think one thing is better and another thing is worse. That's not how it is. Don't worry about everything, just worry about yourself.

Ego is not something to worry about. Why worry about something that is so wonderful and useful? And anyway, what harm can it do? It's just a way to get around and then you drop it and go on without it, or get a different one maybe, I don't know how it works. Maybe this time you are the good guy and next time you are the bad guy. It's just what you do, so what? Who cares, right? Well, you do, I would say. That's the magic part.

That's what I'm hearing now, ego wants to do some great thing that means having no ego. Does it make sense that ego wants to have no ego? No, it makes no sense. It's crazy, but that's what ego is good for, to be crazy. It's not easy to be crazy without ego. Being crazy is not bad, but thinking crazy is bad is good. Did I say that right? Whatever doesn't make sense makes sense once you see things right by not seeing them wrong. Everything makes good sense even if you don't think so. That's a good tip.

You have the wrong idea about ego. You think you and ego are the same thing. That's okay, that's a part of it sometimes, but sometimes not, right? Sure, sometimes yes, sometimes no, that's the way. It's okay as long as it's okay, but when it gets to be not okay then it's not okay, right? Then maybe you want to give it some thought, maybe do something, like maybe you're doing now, coming here. If you weren't here, I wouldn't be talking to you.

Ego is just another word for who you think you are, which is not who you really are. Maybe you don't think so because you think you are a real person with many qualities. Real self is the I and the I has no qualities, so if there are qualities, then that is not the real self. That is pretend self. That is just who you are in coma. You have to be someone, I guess.

You are convinced that you are you, so for me to say you are not you is not a natural thought for you to understand. When someone talks about being free from attachment, this is the only attachment that matters, the attachment to pretend self. They might not tell you that in all the traditions if they don't know or if they want you to join them or something. Their real job is just to give you something to do and they really don't tell you that. I'm not sure they know.

Why be against your ego? That's like being against your body or your house or your car or something. It makes no sense. Ego is not a problem, ego is wonderful. The problem is just where you think you are the pretend self when you are the thing behind it. Ego is not bad, you are just wrong because you think ego is who you are, but ego is just like something you wear for a little while and then you take it off and let it go. You can be attached to it but you don't have to be.

You think maybe someone is further along because they have no attachment with ego or they have a title or some other thing, but no one is further along. There is no such thing as that. How can there be? In truth, everyone is exactly the same, even now, even if you don't know it. Someone else might seem better, but not in a real sense, just in a coma sense. That difference is a feature of coma only. You might think it would be better to be some other self, but it's your self that has that idea, not really you. You feel one way but you can think another.

You can see here I have an ego, so what? What would I look like without an ego? Nothing, right? What's the big thing about an ego? Just don't worry about it. Try worrying about other things and let ego just do its job. It will take care of itself, even more than you want. Try to just worry about real stuff and let the fake stuff worry about itself.

The Cross of the Moment

> We would rather be ruined than changed,
> We would rather die in dread
> Than climb the cross of the moment
> And let our illusions die.
>
> *W. H. Auden*

B ACK IN THE DAY, as they say, during the few
short years when I was playing the absurd role of
spiritual teacher and sharing the stage with those playing the absurd role of spiritual seeker, I experimented
with different ways of saying things and watching to
see how they were received. Even before I understood
it myself, those students were basically my guinea pigs
for the books to come.

I would try out new metaphors, some of which weren't great, others of which were surprisingly good. I would polish anecdotes and parables. I would watch to see what got through people's defenses, what bounced off, and especially, what seemed to penetrate but didn't. I watched to see how ego responded to different messages; testing its defenses and seeing which approaches brought which reactions. That's what I was doing, that's what I was getting out of it. I thought I was just polishing my act, but it was all about the books.

Much of what I said to students was obviously going in one ear and out the other. They might sit and nod and agree, but it was clear that they were completely impervious to any message that might threaten to undermine the structure of the ego-self. Some messages, I learned, would be instantly converted from an assault *against* their egoic structure to a reinforcement *of* it, as if I was throwing rocks that they would then use to shore up their walls. That's how ego works, and ego is very interesting to me. That's what I enjoyed about the whole teaching thing; studying ego's survival prowess and adaptability. Any fullscale frontal attack will always be swept effortlessly aside, but those probing assaults were an interesting way to perform an exploration of ego's marvelous defensive capabilities.

Eventually, I realized that what I said to students didn't really matter much. The only thing that might make a difference was getting a message through to the Little Bastard within. There's no point in trying to convince ego to kill itself; the whole idea of ego seeking truth is, as the entire history of human spirituality shows, a non-starter. But there is an internal insurgency inside every seeker – small, weak, uninformed, unarmed – and that's who you have to get a message to if you want to get something going. Ego will never willingly deconstruct itself, but the Little Bastard might gain enough traction to rise up and tear down the egoic structure from within. Probably not, of course, but when it does work, when Maya does get toppled, that's how it happens; this small inner spark somehow becomes a blaze.

Spiritual seekers can be pretty crazy people. The most dedicated of them will undergo all sorts of hardship in their search for whatever they're searching for; they'll starve, freeze, get whacked with a stick, give away money and possessions, contort themselves into pretzels, endure mind-numbing boredom, travel to foreign lands to consume mystically-flavored swill and much more, but the one thing they *won't* do is turn inward. Ego convinces them that they *are* inward-facing, but they really aren't so no progress is made. Going inward is a process of self-annihilation, whereas virtually all spiritual aspirants are pursuing some form of self-improvement. As long as they can stay pointed outward and feel that they're making progress toward some imagined ideal, they'll put up with anything, but the only thing that can ever make a difference is turning inward, and that's what no one ever does.

In my experience, those who do venture inward and do what is necessary to dismantle the ego-self from within are not really in student mode. They're always off on their own trip in their own space. They may be in the vicinity of a teacher, but once you've begun the real process of awakening you don't need anyone else for anything, just as once you've fallen off a cliff you don't need your trail map anymore.

"My practice is from the great Ramana Maharshi," she tells me. "I do the self-inquiry. I ask myself repeatedly, Who am I? Who am I? All the time, even now, in the back of my mind this is repeating. Who am I? Who am I? Like a machine I can't turn off."

"And how's that going for you?" I ask.

"I don't think it's going for me very good," she snaps.

"That's because it's a trick question," I reply. "You ask yourself who you are in order to peel away the layers of self, but self is all layers and nothing else. No-self is true self. Self-inquiry is not a process of self-discovery but of self-deconstruction."

"Oh no," she says, "that doesn't sound so good."

❊

She'd been living in the house for awhile and had recently started to accompany me during my morning walks which took some effort on her part because, due to my off-kilter sleep habits, my mornings tended to come at all hours and several times a day. English was not her first language, but she spoke it pretty well.

The practice of self-inquiry, of asking "Who am I?", ultimately leads to the realization that self is not the destination of the spiritual journey. But if self is not real, then what is it that searches? And why? What's the point if not for self-improvement or self-evolution or self-salvation? And why, why, *why* give up the lovely illusion of selfhood for the pointless reality of no-self?

To answer my own question, there are only two reasons for seeking to awaken from the dreamstate: The first and most common stems from egoic motivations which can never possibly succeed, but which enjoy all manner of support from the spiritual marketplace. The other reason, and the only way that *can* succeed, is if you somehow develop a searing white-hot hatred for bullshit so intense that you would eagerly hurl yourself into an active volcano rather than continue picnicking on its slopes.

This is where self-inquiry takes you, to the top of the sacred mountain only to discover not a lofty pinnacle but a dark empty hole. It's a process of progressive disillusionment as layer after layer of personal identity collapse under the weight of scrutiny, leaving, of course, nothing.

※

She uses common Sanskrit words liberally, but the only foreign terms I have any use for are Brahman, Atman, and Maya. I like Annica, Anatta, and Anavastha, but I don't use them much because it's easier to just say impermanence, no-self, and it's turtles all the way down. The thing to remember about all that ancient Eastern stuff is that there's no one on the other end who has a firm grip on any of it. There's no one out there in the mystical fog who can figure this stuff out better than you can, and what if there was? You're stuck with you, right here, right now. Seekers are drawn to ancient traditions in their search for answers, but they just get sucked in and bogged down, probably permanently. For ego, that's victory.

※

"I come here to discover myself," she says, "to learn about myself, to understand myself better."

That's what she said when I asked why she was there. It was a common response, but it was not something I could help with.

"There is no self to discover or understand," I say. "Self is a fiction, so there's nothing to discover or learn about."

"Oh," she says, "this is very bad news."

I didn't know if she meant no-self or that she was talking to the wrong guy.

"The self you imagine yourself to be is really just a tumbleweed, a bird's nest, a dust bunny," I say.

"And what is this dust bunny?" she asks.

"Those little balls of dust and cobwebs that hide behind doors and under beds."

"Oh no," she exclaims. "That's what I am? But that is no good!"

"That's all anyone really is. That's what self is. Just a random collection of debris that builds up and turns into the unique little snowflake of you. You didn't create yourself, you are not the author of your character, so what is it about yourself that you take so personally?"

"But there must be something. I am me!"

We are walking down an overgrown road leading to a nice little lake surrounded by trees and a path. There's a small weedy beach with a bench. We sit. I would feed the ducks but I have nothing for them which is okay because there are none so they're not hungry.

"You know what a paper mache mask is?" I ask.

"With the balloon and the paste and the little bits of newspaper," she replies.

"Yes, it's a good analogy for the self you were hoping to discover. You start out with a balloon, which is like an artificially segregated bit of the environment, just as the ego-self is an artificially segregated bit of consciousness, okay?"

"Yes, okay."

I can always tell when someone says okay too fast, but I press on.

"So you start as a blank. Then someone, your parents mainly, start dipping strips of newspaper in the paste and applying them to the balloon. Still good?"

"Yes," she says uncertainly. "I did this as a child."

"And that's how you come into being as a person, isn't it? How we all do. Over time, layer upon layer, the accumulated layers hardening and giving you your distinctive shape. Some of mom's cigarette ash gets into the paste, some of dad's scotch. The mask gets dropped and dented, decorated, marked up, the nose gets bent, a fly gets stuck and pasted over, whatever. Imperfections and blemishes occur and become a part of you. Other influences come into play, especially while you're still soft and gooey. Slowly, your mask develops from a blank balloon into a unique ego-self. So, like a bird's nest or a dustbunny or a tumbleweed, self is just a semi-random collection of debris. With this in mind, based on what do you identify with the mask of the ego-self?"

"Based on I don't know," she replies. "But this is *me*, this is who I *am*. I cannot be someone else."

"Your self has nothing to do with any real or authentic you because there is no such thing as a real or authentic you. What was there before the paste and newspaper? What's there after? There is no true you in there anywhere, only the accumulated layers of debris."

"This is not very pleasing," she says. "And of the many great teachers of I have known, I believe that exactly zero have called me a bunny of dust."

Epiphanies and realizations are a useful part of the awakening process, but they are nothing in and of themselves. They are like firebombs you possess, but what's the point of having bombs you don't use? To get any benefit from them you have to throw them at stuff, blow stuff up, burn stuff down, that stuff being, of course, the stuff of which you and your dreamstate universe are made. That's how you figure out what burns and what doesn't, and in the dreamstate, everything except I Am burns.

Nonduality provides us with a good example of a commonly possessed but unthrown bomb. It seems like many seekers develop a strong conceptual understanding of not-two, but that understanding is just a tool, a device. Now you must throw it through the windows of your mind and see what it can do, and it can do a lot.

From what I can tell, though, many people who have acquired this bomb would prefer to hold onto it rather than use it, which means that ego has intercepted the bomb and kept it safely out of the hands of the Little

Bastard within who wouldn't hesitate to use it. I would go so far as to say that anyone with a simple theoretical grasp of nonduality – the certainty of one and certain impossibility of zero and two – has all they need to burn their ego structure to the ground. The concept of not-two is very powerful, so if you possess this bomb and you're not either awake or in the throes of internal upheaval, then it never got into the right hands.

"My sense is that you are not right about this," she says. "I understand what you say about the paper mache and influences and all of that, but maybe not so much about the balloon, okay? The balloon is not just nothing, I don't think. The balloon is maybe the soul, yes? To me, this makes much more sense. So okay, maybe I am going through self-inquiry working down through layers of paste and paper that is not the real self, but I would say there is something under all that, and I would say the great spiritual masters would agree with me. The true self is the soul; that is that part you call a balloon of nothing, so you are wrong."

That's what we like to think, that the balloon of artificially segregated consciousness at the core of self is true self or higher self or soul or something. That's the fiction that the process of self-inquiry serves to unmask, deflate, pop. She's insisting that the core self is real because that's where she's at in her own process. She has dug down through many layers of self and is now in the vicinity of the core lie of true self. I know she's not a humorless person, but she's at a very humorless stage.

We cannot discover, uncover or recover our true self because it's not covered, it's nonexistent. This is why we are determined to focus on outward, self-based pursuits like devotion, compassion, knowledge, understanding, practice, tradition, and so on; we will do anything not to turn inward. We want to create and preserve, but to awaken we must destroy. Our desperate need to externalize an internal process is why we have the many-faceted global spiritual marketplace devoted to meeting our every need, whereas the real process of detaching from the ego-self is one of independence and self-sufficiency.

"When working with paper mache," I muse, "the balloon just shrivels up and falls out the hole in the bottom of the mask, right? That hole in the bottom of the mask is the black hole within, the thing we have to deny or cover or disguise because it's a dead giveaway; it's the gateway from the illusion of the segregated self to the reality of infinite consciousness, the glaring plothole in the story of you. That hole is where we're all going eventually, but for as long as we wish to maintain the illusion of self, the black hole must be denied. That's what the spiritual marketplace offers, ways of avoiding the black hole within, but here you are, heading right toward it."

"I don't think that's what I want to do," she says.

"Of course you don't. No one *wants* to. It can't be wanted because there is no *it* to want. You're walking into emptiness."

"And so I must have these obstructions that hide this emptiness at the center of me, or make me forget it or something. This is what you are saying?"

"In essence, the mask of the ego-self is the artificial structure walling us off from the reality of no-self. Self itself is the obstruction, the structure of denial. Self doesn't *have* a black hole, it *is* a black hole. Waking up is not a scholarly pursuit, or even a spiritual one, and there is no secondary objective. Wake up or die trying, that's the name of the game. All spiritual activity boils down to two things; you're either killing the false self or you're just killing time."

"That's not what I hope to hear," she says. "It is alarming to think that I am not me, but I am the one who is alarmed which proves I exist which means there's nothing to be alarmed about."

"Nice try," I say. "The ego-self you believe yourself to be, that you believe to be you, that you think of as 'me', is nothing. It is made of nothing, it means nothing, and it ends up as nothing. It's a brief spark in the infinite night. It is not you because there is no you. There is a truth of you, but you are not it."

"This infinite spark in the brief night shit sounds all wrong to me," she says, heating up a bit. "This is something anyone could say. Oh, there is no you. Oh, you don't even exist. Oh, you are just this mask, this paper mache piece of garbage and when you are done with it there is nothing left of you. Anyone can say such a thing, but obviously I am real. Obviously there is a real me. This means you are not right about what you are saying."

"Then prove me wrong. All you have to do to prove I'm wrong about everything is prove anything, and I'll have to go out and get a regular job."

"Yes, yes, you would be very nice at the grocery store pushing in the carts, or in the tiny booth where I pay for parking. You make a nice situation for yourself, saying to people things they can't argue with. I see this, I see how this works. But maybe you should try some new material someday, okay? Because this no, no, no is making me very tired. Maybe you say yes to something, maybe you say something nice like love is real or we are all in a common cause, I don't know, but something nice, okay? You can't just say no to everything. It's very negative."

Ego is a marvelous thing to behold. There is nothing more worthy of our respect and admiration. Nothing in the dreamstate compares to Maya because Maya *is* the dreamstate. We are in Maya's house and living under her rules and the very belief that we're not is the gravitational force that holds us on the dreamstage playing out our empty little dramas.

All that any so-called teacher can really do to get past egoic fortifications and help a student wake up is broadcast a message from outside the walls of the ego-self. If someone inside is awake and eager for change and actively listening, then maybe the message gets through and something comes of it. And that's what's going on right here, right now, right? I am outside your walls broadcasting this message. Are you actively listening? Are you eager for change? I'm not saying you should be, just that you might want to ask your-self what you're doing right now.

"To be no-self is not making me happy," she says as we continue our stroll. "Everyone in the past, all these many teachers, they said I was supposed to discover my true self. That's what I thought I was doing, and that love was a part of it also, and maybe some bliss. Now I have to wonder, if it's right what you say, what am I doing?"

"Once you understand that you are not the character you inhabit, then the question becomes; If I'm not the self, what am I? And why am I doing this spiritual stuff? If there's no *me* to benefit, then what's the point of any of it?"

"And? Yes? What is the answer to this?"

"Obviously, there is no point. There is no benefit to arriving at no-self because there's no self left to enjoy any benefit. If you want to keep your ego and be a student or teacher in the dreamstate, then the spiritual marketplace will let you have your cake and eat it too, but if you follow the trajectory of awakening you will find a black hole at the end of the rainbow, and your only consolation will be that you are no longer a lie."

"But then there is not even a me to say I am not a lie."

"Right."

"So then a lie is all I am now?"

"Of course. This is the dreamstate; the whole thing is a fictional production like a stageplay, and you have accepted it as real and mistaken yourself for your character."

"But if I am not this character, then I am the actor that plays the character."

"That would just be another layer of self to penetrate and dismantle. The truth is that there is no actor, there is only the character. The mask is hollow. This is where people like to conjure up a higher self or oversoul or something, but the same questions still apply and the same dismantling is still required, so you keep peeling the onion only to discover it's all layers and no core. Turtles upon turtles."

"I don't feel very much like an onion or a turtle," she says. "I think you are saying things just to upset me. Is this your procedure? I have known many teachers with many procedures. One teacher would just sit there and stare at me for a very long time. What am I to do? Stare back? Cry? Fall asleep? I don't like that woman at all. Another one kept asking about when I was a little girl, get a lot of emotion going, make a lot of hugging. I know that trick. One teacher wanted me to give him free massage all the time, like he was doing me a favor. Some teachers I have liked but maybe for bad reasons. I am not liking you too much as a teacher right now."

"Then I guess I'm doing my job."

"Yes, yes, thank you for some more clever talk which I really don't need."

As soon as your ego-self detects a threat, it diverts you over to some self-preserving activity. If the threat continues, an army of parasitic emotional demons will be dispatched into your heart and mind to lay siege to your thoughts and feelings. Fear and dread will turn your heart heavy and twist your guts and put you in a fight-or-flight mode. This is why we are so relieved to find spiritual teachers who are positive and light and sing a happy song about peace and love, and give us easy-to-follow instructions; we are mortally sickened by any threat to the ego-self.

I have been called a nihilist, which means that I view life as meaningless, which I obviously do because it obviously is, but that doesn't mean that life is without purpose. Life, the dreamstate, *you*, are meaningless but purposeful, just as games and art are meaningless but purposeful. Even the illusion of meaning has purpose. You don't need to know what your purpose is, but you can be sure it's meaningless. The purpose of the ego-self, like it or not, is to amuse the sole beholder, just as the purpose of the dream is to amuse the dreamer.

"What's true of you is what's true of anyone," I say, "meaning that you could be anyone in the same way you are you, so who is this self you want to discover? It's just one paper mache mask out of infinite possible variations; random, haphazard, created without your authentic input because at no point has there existed an authentic you. So if you're not you, who are you?"

"I am just asking myself that again and again. Who am I? Who am I? This is my practice," she says. "This is from Ramana Maharshi. Maybe you've heard of him?"

"You've been doing the self-inquiry for a long time, right?"

"A long time I would say, yes," she says.

"And you have discovered that all sorts of things you thought were real but really weren't, right?"

"That's all that has happened so far," she says.

"And that's all that's *supposed* to happen. That means the process is working. Now you're confused because you have arrived at a point where there doesn't seem to be any other possible answer to the question, Who am I?, right?"

"It's like knocking on doors but now there are no more doors to knock."

"Which is the real point of self-inquiry, to come to the realization that there is no self. That's where you are now, trying to process a discovery that doesn't make any sense to you. Spiritual dissonance."

"But I have made no discovery. If you were listening you would know this."

"You have discovered that there is nothing to discover. You are getting close to the bottom of self and finding it empty. You are beginning to confront your inner black hole."

"Yes, well, as a teacher I think you are not very good. Maybe you should think more about that regular job. Sell popcorn at the movies, maybe. Tell people your great wisdom while you pour on the fake butter."

That's basically all I'm doing anyway.

"But now you're asking me," I say, "so I'm telling you, self does not hold the answer to the riddle of being. Knowing yourself is not enlightenment because your self is a fiction. The self-inquiry practice isn't meant to help you discover true self but the truth of no-self."

"This is not what my other teachers have said," she says. "They have told me there is a true self and that when I have truly arrived then my experience will be of unconditional love, yes? Then I will be free of suffering and my heart will be wide open."

"Anything you've been taught just adds to the accumulated blockage you must now dislodge if you want to move forward. This means you have to make a conscious decision to stop adding to the blockage and focus on clearing your pipes. In the end, the whole process of awakening is really just a simple plumbing challenge."

"Merde," she says.

"Exactly. All this accumulated shit has built up in hardened layers that backs you up and reduces your energetic flow to a tiny trickle. The more of this obstruction you manage to remove, the more you expand to your rightful dimensions. No knowledge is required unless it acts as a tool to unclog your pipes. The whole thing is just a matter of clog-busting, whereas the role of most teachers and teachings in the spiritual marketplace is to create, protect and reinforce the clogs. That's a valid and necessary dreamstate function, but here we're talking about something else."

"If what you say is right, then I am very wrong about everything," she says. "This would come as a great disappointment."

"Of course you're wrong about everything," I reply. "Everyone is wrong about everything all the time, it's the defining feature of life in the dreamstate. You can never be true in a false context, and all context is false. The dreamstate is simply an artificial context, like a theater or a video game. Self can't become true, but it can become progressively less and less false, which is what you're doing now, which is why you're experiencing discomfort."

We walk in silence while she, I assume, contemplates my sagely words, and while I try to think of a ten letter word for dyspepsias, third, fourth, eighth and tenth letter 's'.

"I tell you, I don't especially enjoy discomfort," she says sternly, as if I were the cause.

"Then you're talking to the wrong guy."

"Well then, maybe I should be talking to the *right* guy, right? Maybe I should be talking to the guy who is not telling me there is no me, because I can tell you, that makes no sense to me."

"Anger is good, but don't waste it on me."

"You don't have to tell me not to waste my anger," she says. "I have plenty for everyone. Seven years of this and what do I have? I have nothing!"

"Nothing is actually the goal, but you're not there yet. There's still a you to have nothing. You still have you, but now you're finding out, thanks to self-inquiry, that you don't even have that. This spiritual stuff may not go where you thought, but you've gone a long way."

We continue our walk. For my amusement and to give her something neutral to focus on, I deliver a short talk on what Sartre called bad faith, what Camus called philosophical suicide, and what I call abdication. In all three cases, it means relinquishing our self-sovereignty to some non-self agent or agency because the freedom of finding our own way is way too scary. More accurately, we're afraid of going inward and will jump at any excuse to turn the journey outward. We can point to Buddhism and New Age spirituality as clear examples of pandering to this self-preservation urge. Another good example is probably whatever you're doing right now.

We don't want freedom and we don't want to take responsibility for ourselves. Medicine, religion, government and basically all institutions, exist to allow us to abdicate responsibility for ourselves to others so we can relax in our safe, cozy little cells and feel content in the belief, based mainly on decorative elements and a *trompe l'oeil* design scheme, that we are in control of our lives. It is essential to both the human condition and a functioning dreamstate that we fear and abhor even the slightest whiff of freedom. It is the worst possible thing; a thing to be glamorized and desired but never achieved. (Unless you're in an actual jail cell or some other shitty confines, then freedom is obviously a good thing to desire.)

Of course, my standing disclaimer applies: I speak in the context of awakening from delusion to an assumed audience of truth-seekers, or, at least, to those with an active interest in the reality of enlightenment. It is only in the context of awakening that being wrong is wrong. In any other context, being wrong is perfectly right, with not the slightest hint of irony or judgment intended. Normal people are perfectly correct to eschew freedom, to burn any heretic who threatens them with it, to take sanctuary in their cells and pretend they're not free to leave. That's what life is, that's how it works, that's what you're supposed to do. Those who do otherwise, who venture dangerously inward rather than safely outward, are the cheaters, the malcontents, the ones who would rather hack the game than play it, regardless of the cost.

In my experience, virtually all spiritual seekers insist on looking without for what lies within. That's why students are never qualified to ask questions and why I stopped playing the teacher role. The teacher-student dynamic is inherently inoperable unless both parties are in the outward mode which, in the spiritual marketplace, is usually the case.

"Imagine a bonsai master," I tell her, "the best one ever. The all-time grandmaster of bonsai, okay."

"And bonsai is what? The dinky tree thing?"

"Yes, the Japanese art of dinky trees. Now the Bonsai master is old and bearded, very sagely and very wise, but he didn't start out that way. He was once young and clever and determined, just like you are now. Being clever and determined is perfectly okay, but it's also how you find your way out of the funhouse, which is not okay. This young man wasn't just some

New Age interior designer, this was a guy who was actually going to get up and go, and that's what he actually did, but it didn't actually get him anywhere because his cleverness and determination were safely rerouted into the gentle art of micro-shrubbery. Thus, a viable threat to ego has been averted and the show goes on."

"Meaning, according to you, that this man's lifetime of focus and dedication, and his mastery of his art, is all of no value?"

"Exactly. It's a within-the-dreamstate activity. It does not lead out. That's the only thing that matters."

"And it means nothing that he is a great sage? That he is very wise?"

"Of course not. Again, his status is within the dreamstate. He is just another of infinite variations of the ego-self, in no way better or worse than any other. Just another paper-mache mask; that's the only distinction we need to recognize."

"And who is the mastermind behind this great deception?" she asks. "Who is saving your bonsai man from his dangerous youthful urges?"

"His ego, of course, which is to say, he has saved himself, or his self has saved itself, or Brahman saved Atman, something like that. In any event, the bonsai guy never stood much chance against himself."

"And so who is the winner of such a contest?" she demands.

"The bonsai guy wins because he was setting himself on a pointless path of self-destruction, but was saved to live a life of purpose and drama. As a young man, he was exercising the power of focus, which poses an existential threat to the ego-self, so his focus was gently shifted to something safe. He was protected against a tendency toward escape, and went on to live an amused and amusing life in his little cell with his little trees; a big fish in a small pond instead of a non-fish in an infinite pond. The life-purpose for which he was saved was meaningless, yes, but all purpose is meaningless; cure cancer, raise children, write spiritual books, save the world, groom little trees, polish turds, all the same, all safe and meaningless little microdramas. Meaning is off the table, so the illusion of meaning must suffice. It's all just drama for the sake of drama."

"And I am now on this pointless path of self-destruction? This is what you are saying?"

"I'm saying that your ego-self is trying to save itself from a pointless path of self-destruction, and you're fighting it. You're drowning and you're fighting off your rescuer. I'm asking if that's what you really want to do."

"And you are my wonderful rescuer?"

"Oh no, I'm very happy to watch you struggle and drown. It's your ego and the teachers it has selected that are trying to save you."

"But I chose self-inquiry."

"Thinking it led to true self. Your Little Bastard tricked you into discovering no-self."

"Oh, thank you Little Bastard, how nice that now I get to drown. This is what the self-inquiry process threatens me with?"

"As with all questions, self-inquiry doesn't lead to an answer, but to the destruction of the question. The question is, Who am I?, and the answer is, no one. You peel away the paper mache mask of self, looking for true self, but whether you tear the mask apart in tiny strips or big chunks, you must eventually arrive at the discovery that there is nothing inside. You are coming into this phase of discovery right now."

We follow a narrow treeline between dormant fields. Crows are pretending not to watch us. I have a thing for crows, but if they ever grow thumbs the time of man will be over.

After walking in silence for awhile, I sense that she needs to be distracted from her thoughts, so I play with the paper mache analogy some more.

"You can decorate your mask, which is what most people do. This involves modifying how you are perceived by others, or rather, how you perceive you are perceived by others. Make yourself pretty, clever, powerful, rich, have stuff, have position, all that."

"Which is all just vanity, yes?"

"Everything outward is vanity, yes, self-fulfilling selfhood. You can also groom yourself for the unseen seer, which is the agent or agency we feel is watching us, judging us. Even when we don't give it a name like God or Allah or mother or Big Brother, most of us have this sense that we are under scrutiny at all times. This is just another type of audience member we can direct our performance to, as if by believing we are being seen, we can believe that we exist, and that we are as we imagine ourselves to be."

"I did not make sense of that last part," she says.

"We need to believe we have an audience," I try again, "like a vanity mirror. We are naturally incapable of self-validating, so we must get that validation from others, even if we have to imagine those others, and that they see us as we wish to be seen."

"This gets very tricky, I see," she says.

"Making sense of the ego-self gets tricky, but it's just an idle pastime for leisurely walks. It doesn't matter how the false works, only that it's false. There's never any reason to dissect and examine the obstructions that spiritually constipate us, only to blast through each one and move onto the next."

"This is going nowhere I like," she says.

"Which is yet another belief you might want to loosen your grip on, the bliss myth; this whole idea that freedom and happiness walk hand in hand. The key to happiness is comfortable constraint, not freedom. We believe that freedom is happiness, but we fear actual freedom like we fear death. The infrastructure of the false self is rigid containment; the mask, the cell. Someone once said that life is largely a matter of burrows, and that's the truth of the egoic being. The artificial nature of the ego-self requires specificity in size and shape, in time and space, in belief and understanding. The dimensions of one's cell are the dimensions of one's being because they're really the same thing. The paper mache mask of the ego-self does not reside within a cell, it *is* the cell. Ego is a set of false confines, but truth hath no confines. What is an inflated balloon if you take away the rubber part? Both nothing and everything, right?"

"This is a lot to take in," she says. "I don't see how such a thing as ego can even hold together."

"Emotion is the paste. Emotionally charged beliefs are all a person is, and all of your beliefs can be flipped like a switch or burned to ash, so again, what is there about you to call you? The ego-self is a collection of opinions and beliefs held together by the binding agent of emotional energy. When that runs out, this paper mache mask of the ego-self collapses back into the nothingness from whence it came; garbage to garbage, trash to trash."

Here's what enlightenment and death look like in this metaphor. When the mask of the ego-self is destroyed, there is a period during which the segregated awareness that was inside the shell maintains its shape and coherence, as if it was emotional energy that held it together rather than the shell, or the shell was really just an emotional forcefield in the first place. When the structural containment of the ego-mask is removed, the dissipation of finite awareness back into infinite consciousness is not immediate. The segregated awareness that had been isolated within the mask loses its shape slowly, like an iceberg melting back into the ocean. That's where I am now, well along in the process of reintegration with the whole. I have lost all my edges and sharp points. I am rounded and smooth, following currents and floating on the tide. I have lost both the individuation of the mask and the shape of the balloon. And yet, by undergoing the process of awakening from the dreamstate while still in-body, I have only managed to accelerate the natural process of reintegration which any ego-self must eventually undergo; the loss of artificial definition.

And that's what death is too, I suppose. The vehicle of the physical self is eliminated, and then, over time, the emotional cohesion of the ego-self dissipates. Maybe this explains ghosts; ego-selves that have lost their bodies but still retain some degree of emotional coherence. Maybe that's why they linger for awhile; those with strong emotional energy in the form of powerful connections or unresolved issues.

Well, you can do it the other way too, with the ego-self dying and the body staying alive, and that's what enlightenment is.

There is no such thing as being dead. Dead is not a state of being just as non-being is not a state of being, just as zero is not a number. You might think that some part of you survives forever, and you're right, but that part of you is perfectly impersonal so your immortality isn't really yours. Think of the paper mache mask. Take away the hardened bits of encrusted debris and what's left? What's left when the mask is gone is what was there before it was created. You can call it infinite consciousness or truth, but you can't call it *you* because there was no you before the mask and there is no you after. You are just an artificially segregated unit of infinite awareness, temporarily isolated and defined by the short-lived emotional coherence of the ego-mask.

"I wonder if I need a new practice," she says. "Asking who am I all the time gets no answer anymore."

"You can only make so much progress in your monkey-mind," I reply. "It's time to move your practice out of your head and onto paper. Write it out. That in-your-head stuff is either for illiterate populations or to bring about a subconsciously desired failure. You can think a million times better outside your head than in, like a laser beam compared to a lightbulb."

"Now I don't know how much more thinking I want to do."

"Then that would be a good thing to write out and get clear about. What do you want? On the other hand, you might want to proceed with caution. Your mind, when you really start using it, is like a flamethrower that you can't control. What do you think a flamethrower does in a world made of veils? Things can get pretty crazy pretty fast."

"Flamethrowers, laserbeams, firebombs, little bastards; okay with me," she says. "I don't care anymore what gets out of hand. I am getting very tired of no results. Everything so far is just more and more nothing, I would like just for once to find something, not more nothing."

"Try the writing," I suggest, "even at random, just to see where it goes. Start with one thing and let it turn into another, let it become whatever it wants. You don't have to know where to start, just start. You don't have to know where you're going, just go. Begin the process and allow it to take over. When you see something dark and scary, go boldly into it. If you don't like writing, try vocalizing. Go off where you're sure you'll be alone and unheard, and talk and rail and rant and question and demand and primal scream and just let out whatever wants to come out."

"Now it sounds like I am at the very beginning once again."

"Get used to it. This is a journey of steps. When you finish one, you come to the beginning of the next. Each step is a complete process and, as I recall, none of them are a lot of fun."

Will vocalizing work for her? I don't know. It worked for Brett who we saw in *Warfare*. Her whole process seemed to be about walking around a pond, ranting and raving against whatever came before her, slaying demons, tossing bombs, cursing, screaming, killing her father, thinking as hard as she could. Pondering, I suppose we have to call it. And after however many months or years it took, she was Done.

Will the process of Spiritual Autolysis work for you? I don't know. I would think it would work for most seekers in one session or less because most seekers don't really have much burning discontent, just a kind of egoic desire to be enlightened because it sounds cool, like the spiritual counterpart of a fast car or a bikini body. Do you wish to generate a discontent you don't currently feel? Why? If your Little Bastard is asleep, let him sleep. If he's waking up, you'll be hearing from him soon enough. Spiritual Autolysis, written or vocal, is a way of processing something that wants to come out. If you're not burning from the inside, then you don't need to process anything. Nothing is at risk and it's not now or never. It's not true that there's no time like the present; *all* time is like the present. If you don't have to do it, why mess with it? There's no upside.

Human Adulthood, on the other hand, is *all* upside. Unlike enlightenment, the Integrated State makes sense and is universally desirable.

Whatever it is you want to accomplish – enlightenment, integration, or just an internal cleansing – I would say it all starts the same way; you have to go inward and perform a deep housecleaning. Spiritual autolysis is how you think better and how you bring the mind more fully into alignment through focus and coherence, which is the only way you will stand a chance against emotion. You don't need a therapist or meds or a support group or even friends. Purge out some emotional-vomit letters to your parents, write hate-mail to God, forgive your trespassers or beg the forgiveness of those you've trespassed against. The point isn't to heal or forgive or find redemption or open your heart, it's to process clogged mental-emotional debris out of your system so you can emerge from the pre-born state into the self-born state where you can live authentically. If you are backed up with unprocessed mental-emotional debris, no matter how far it's stuffed down, you have to hawk it up and spit it out, or get it out however it'll come; write, scream, sweat, shit, puke, who cares? The only thing that matters is getting rid of it. You have to forcibly expel old beliefs and feelings or you will be forever stuck at the prepubescent stage of development you're probably stuck at right now, and regardless of whatever else you might achieve in life, you will never have truly been alive because you will have stopped developing before your emergence into your rightful state of being.

I've said it many times. That's why you're here, that's what you really want. That's why you're reading this. Integration is like a mini-enlightenment or pre-enlightenment, and it's probably the state of the authentic mystic. There's a price to be paid, of course, but after you let go of what must be released, you see that it was never really yours anyway, so the price was really nothing. Gateless gate and all that.

Those who are not reborn from flesh to spirit are not born at all, and if this applies to you, you can ignore it, deny it, or you can take up the mighty pen and do something about it. You're gonna die anyway, so what the hell. It doesn't matter what you do, of course, and you can't save yourself because there's no self to save, but why not play a good game? Why not swim up and see if you can't break the surface?

It's a whole different world up there.

As an interesting epilogue to this story, the woman with whom I shared those walks years ago was one of several I was privileged to assist on a successful journey. Her name was Marichelle.

Starship Gita

Act 6: Enlightenment

The bridge returns to normal lighting. The Borg Queen peels off her mask and becomes the Director. She starts slapping Picard/Patrick and yelling at him.

DIRECTOR
(slapping and shaking him)
Wake up! Patrick! Patrick! Wake up! What's wrong with you? Patrick!

PICARD/PATRICK
(confused, anxious)
What? Patrick? I know that name. You mean… you mean I'm not really Captain Jean-Luc Picard?

DIRECTOR
Of course not, Patrick, you're an actor. Picard is just the role you're playing. Your character.

PICARD/PATRICK

And this isn't really the Enterprise?

DIRECTOR

This? It's just a soundstage on a studio lot.

PICARD/PATRICK

Then Geordi was right? We're not really on the verge of a terrible war?

DIRECTOR

Of course we are, in the script. What's wrong with you, Patrick? Did you get so far into character that you forgot who you really are?

PICARD/PATRICK

But Q! The Borg Queen! It was all so real!

DIRECTOR

Look Patrick, you had a psychotic break, it happens to actors. We get so immersed in a character that we forget who we really are. But now I need you to come back and remember what's going on so we can finish out the scene. I am not Maya or Q or Krishna or the Borg Queen, I am your director, Patrick, your friend and colleague. I am not here to set you free, but to remind you of who you really are; an actor in a dramatic production. I need you to stand up and start this war. Red alert, battle stations, remember?

PICARD/PATRICK
(struggles to his knees)

Yes, yes, I know my lines, but how do I know this is real? Why should I think Patrick is any more real than Picard? What makes *this* world more real than another? This is just another layer, another veil that must be ripped away. Now is the time! I must take action or fall forever back into the endless gloom of the unawakened mind!

Picard seizes the Director by the throat. He rises to his feet as he chokes her. She resists. In a pillar of light she morphs back into Borg Queen. He continues strangling her as he speaks.

PICARD

You *are* Maya, Goddess of Illusion! You *are* Shiva, Destroyer of Worlds! You *are* Q the trickster and Krishna the prankster. You *are* the Borg Queen and yes, I am already a drone, I see that now. But the time has come to awaken from this dream. Whatever the cost, I will no longer be deceived! I will do what must be done to end this lie. Whatever the price, I will have the truth!

The Borg Queen slumps. Picard drops her body. He snaps his tunic taut and regains his command demeanor. He faces the two ships on the main screen as he speaks.

PICARD

My illusion is thus dispelled. The Little Bastard that found voice in La Forge now finds a champion in me! Whatever this is, whoever I am, one thing is certain; truth exists and untruth does not. That which is false can be destroyed, but truth can never be harmed!

Now will I, a true son of Solomon, separate fact from fiction through the purifying power of fire! Now will I set torch to everything. Now will I destroy these ships and lay waste these armies. Now will I reduce everything and everyone to ash. The false shall be burned away, only truth shall remain!

This is the day of my right birth, and I will not let fear dissuade me from my duty. If I die, then I was never real and nothing is lost. If I survive, then for the first time will I know truth from lie.

Turns to bridge crew.

Red alert! All hands to battle stations!

The bridge is bathed in pulsing red light. Battle sirens wail. Picard takes his seat in the captain's chair. He presses a button on his console to address the entire ship.

PICARD

Crew of the Enterprise, this is your captain speaking. The time of reckoning has finally arrived. The unthinkable has become the inevitable and the great battle is about to commence. We do not enter this conflict with fearful hearts, but throw our arms wide out to embrace our destiny. This is not a time for fear and trembling, but for joy and great gladness. For too long have we been subject to an inequitable peace. Now, at long last, we choose a just war. Brace for impact!

Releases button. Stands. Snaps tunic taut.

Mr. Data, prepare to ram the Borg ship and detonate the warp core. Mr. Worf, send a subspace message to Starfleet Command: *This is the final report of the USS Enterprise. We have engaged the motherfuckin' Borg.*

Slowly, he smiles.

Mr. Data… engage.

THE END

The Caneless Cane

Fall seven times, stand up eight.

Zen saying

O NE FINE MORNING, long ago in days of yore, before cell phones and internet, a student named Jason approached me to complain that after weeks of diligent effort, he wasn't making any progress. He was actually kind of whiny about it.

I bowed my head in silence for several minutes in order to appear contemplative while wondering if you can really slip on a banana peel, or if that's just a cartoon trope like your eyes popping out when you see a gorgeous dame. After a sagely interval, I allowed my ocean of wisdom to spew forth.

"There are three words in the English language that end in n-g-r-y," I revealed unto Jason. "Pray, tell me what they are."

He got hungry and angry pretty quick, (the words, not the conditions), but then he kind of seized up on the third. I bade him depart.

The next morning Jason approached me again, this time bleary-eyed, slump-shouldered, and a bit overwrought.

"I was up all night," he said in a cracking voice. "I thought about it, I asked people, I even went through the whole dictionary, page by page."

"And?"

"And nothing. I have this thing stuck in my brain, like I just keep making sounds and sticking n-g-r-y on the end to see if it's a word. *Mangry, sangry, fangry, quangry, langry*, I can't make it stop. My brain just keeps doing it, even now, *bongry, wongry, dingry, dongry*. Look, I'm sorry, I tried, I just can't do it. *Smingry, smangry, pingry, pangry*. Can you please just tell me so I can stop obsessing and get some rest?"

I gazed serenely upon Jason as if he was our hope for the future, which he wasn't. I made a church of my hands and put the steeple to my lips because I was experimenting with different wisdom looks. I tried a slight head-tilt left, then right.

"When you went through the dictionary," I said, "did you check the variations? Like angry is a form of anger, hungry is a form of hunger. Did you look at all that, or just the main words?"

His red-rimmed eyes moistened in despair. He groaned unattractively and withdrew from my illustrious presence.

☼

The next morning he reappeared, looking several times worse. He had gone through the entire dictionary again, he moaned, but much more carefully this time, and his brain was still racing madly through an endless torrent of permutations. Still nothing.

"Are you sure you're really trying?" I asked.

"Please," he cried in desperation, "I'm sorry, I just can't do it. *Stongry, congry, dingry, dongry, clangry, flangry.* I don't know what it is. Can you please, *please* just tell me?"

"Tell you what, Jason?"

"The third word!" he barked. "What's the third word that ends in n-g-r-y?"

"Oh, I don't know," I said. "I just overheard the question on the radio a few years ago and I was wondering about it. I thought you might know."

He stared at me rather insanely for a long moment, releasing little puffs of inner turmoil to keep his head from popping off.

"There isn't one," he finally sputtered. "There is no third word, is there?"

"Well, no, I guess you're telling me there's not."

"You knew, didn't you? This whole time, *you knew!*"

"I knew you could make a fuckin' effort, Jason," I replied, "and now, so do you. Go get some rest and come see me tomorrow. I have some other questions for you."

Wisefool Press

Wisefool Press publishes *The Enlightenment Trilogy*, *The Dreamstate Trilogy*, and the *Jed Talks* series by Jed McKenna. Visit WisefoolPress.com to learn more.

Made in the USA
Lexington, KY
27 September 2018